THE
JONSONIAN
MASQUE

THE
JONSONIAN
MASQUE

STEPHEN ORGEL

HARVARD UNIVERSITY PRESS
Cambridge, Massachusetts
1 9 6 5

104440

In Memory of
Paul H. Strauss
and to
Paul J. Alpers

PREFACE

This is an essay on the development of an art form that Ben Jonson made peculiarly his own, and undertakes to consider both what he was working with and what he was attempting to achieve. The masque for Jonson was defined by certain basic requirements — requirements, on the one hand, of his own sensibility and, on the other, of the expectations of his audience. This is my subject: the changing relationship between the masque as spectacle or revel and the masque as literature. To encompass it requires the examination of a good deal of detail, and the six Jonson masques that I discuss at length seem to me to represent crucial moments in Jonson's development of his own idea of the form. My introductory survey of the pre-Jacobean masque is designed not as a history of the genre, but as a discussion of the traditions and conventions within which Jonson was working. My book is not intended, then, as a comprehensive treatment of Jonson's career as a masque writer or as a systematic handbook to his court productions. I can only hope that the limits I have set are sufficiently justified.

The dedication to Paul J. Alpers acknowledges my greatest obligation, but I owe scarcely less to Jonas A. Barish and David M. Kalstone. These three friends have helped at every stage of the work, and I can do no more here than record, in my turn, affection, gratitude, admiration. Of longer standing is my debt to Andrew J. Chiappe, with whom, as a senior at Columbia, I undertook to read all of Jonson. My thinking about the masques has changed greatly since then; nevertheless, Professor Chiappe will recognize here many ideas which were first conceived with his help, and I should add to them a word of tribute to the brilliance and understanding of a great teacher.

Of my professors at Harvard University, I must thank first of all Alfred Harbage, for whom an earlier version of Part Two was written and whose criticism proved most valuable. Douglas Bush helped in innumerable ways throughout my graduate career: a less general acknowledgment to so learned and generous a man would only falsify what I feel I owe him. Most of all I am indebted to Harry Levin and Reuben Brower, with both of whom I worked continuously at Harvard and who served as the two readers of the thesis from which this book developed. Their support extended far beyond the sphere of my studies, and my gratitude and affection similarly extend beyond the bounds of my work here.

To all these I should add the names of a few others. Alan Curtis and Daniel Heartz were my guides through the fields of Renaissance music and dance, and Svetlana Leontief Alpers kindly read the section on the iconography of Comus and made several useful suggestions. Donald Friedman, Susan Gilmore, John Hollander, and Alex Zwerdling have at various points given me the benefit of their encouragement and criticism. My research assistant, Allan Paulson, and my typist, Joan Heifetz, have been admirably patient and capable. Joyce Lebowitz of the Harvard University Press has been a scrupulous and sympathetic editor.

Last, a few corporate acknowledgments: to Harvard for a Dexter Fellowship and to the University of California for a Summer Faculty Fellowship, generous grants that have made my work easier. To the Clarendon Press, publishers of the text of the Oxford *Ben Jonson*, and to the Cambridge University Press, publishers of Albert Feuillerat's edition of Sidney, my thanks for permission to quote. The section on Sidney's *The Lady of May* first appeared in the *Journal of the Warburg and Courtauld Institutes*. To the editors, for permission to reprint it, again my thanks.

Berkeley, California   S. O.
12 July 1964

CONTENTS

ILLUSTRATIONS

following page 150

Figure 1. Hercules' meeting with Virtue and Vice
From Geoffrey Whitney, *Choice of Emblemes* (Leyden, 1586), p. 40.

Figure 2. Comus
From Vincenzo Cartari, *Le Imagini de i Dei degli Antichi* (Lyons, 1581), p. 347.

Figure 3. Comus and revelers
Engraving by Jasper Isaac from Philostratus, *Les Images* (Paris, 1614), p. 9.

Figure 4. Burghers at revels
From Heinrich Assenheim, *Viridarium Hieroglyphico-Morale* . . . (Frankfurt, 1619), p. 132.

The decorations are line adaptations of designs by Inigo Jones for masques at court, in the collection of the Duke of Devonshire, Chatsworth:

Title page: Detail from a pageant car for an unidentified masque.
Part One: The Genius of Floods, for Jonson's *Chloridia*, 1631.
Part Two: Dwarf Lackeys, for the antimasque of *Chloridia*.
Part Three: A Maritime Chariot, for Sir William Davenant's *The Temple of Love*, 1635.

The Metamorphoses of Proteus

NOTE

In quotations I have normalized *u, v, i, j*, the long *s*, and such scribal conventions as superscript letters and contractions.

COURT MASQUES, wrote Ben Jonson, "eyther have bene, or ought to be the mirrors of mans life." [1] But to his collaborator, the great architect and stage designer Inigo Jones, they were "nothing else but pictures with Light and Motion." [2] Jonson implies a very old idea of the function of art, Jones a radical concept of the nature of theater. And though the two positions may not be incompatible, they seemed so to their authors and thus express admirably both the double aspect and the inherent tensions of this uniquely Renaissance form. Most interesting perhaps to the stage historian, the Stuart masque represents a crucial phase in the development of the English theater. Inigo Jones, given a free hand and unlimited funds to realize his most spectacular fantasies, created for King James's Twelfth-Night entertainments what is essentially the modern stage: an instrument for producing a visual illusion of reality. To the spectator of that time, this was something remarkable and largely unfamiliar, contrived out of Italianate devices — moveable settings, perspective scenes, complex machinery — and differing both in kind and degree from the sort of dramatic experience provided by even the most elaborate private playhouses. When this masque stage was finally employed in the production of plays, the effect on the drama was profound and revolutionary.

The masque rightly demands less attention from the student of literature. Nevertheless, Jones created only part of each court production, and it is worth remembering that for over twenty years the creator of another part — the part remaining to us — was a man who declared that the masque was not spectacle, but poetry. How far these two conflicted we know, and the extent of Ben Jonson's quarrel with Jones is a measure of how seriously each artist took his own work. There are, perhaps, enough purely material reasons for Jonson to have written for the court so that we need not ask what attracted him to the form he perfected: for a masque King James gave him five times what his producers paid for a new play. But Jonson's interest in the form went far beyond this, and it is this interest that I propose to examine.

My study will touch on every aspect of Jonson's work on his masques. For when we ask why he should have written twenty-five of these entertainments, we are asking a number of complex questions, only the most superficial of which involves the material attractions of good pay and patronage. We are asking what immediate requirements he was obliged to satisfy by whoever commissioned the productions; but we are also asking what his own art required of him that made him take this form so seriously. We are asking what the conditions of his stage were and how he dealt with them; but we are also asking why he both transcended the Banqueting House at Whitehall and, ultimately, ignored it by insisting that his masques were poems. Finally, we are asking what the tradition of the English masque gave him to work with; but we are also asking how he transformed what he received, to make a living art of a set of conventions.

It is the last that must be considered first, the question of the tradition behind Jonson when, in 1604 (he tells us), he "apted" his invention to the commands of Queen Anne. In analyzing the development of the masque we are concerned not only with what materials — conventions, symbols, formal elements — were available to the poet, but also with what his audience expected a masque to be. The following pages, then, are intended not as a history of the form, but as an attempt to define what constituted a court masque at the beginning of the seventeenth century.

Enid Welsford, concluding her discussion of the Elizabethan masque, provides a useful point of reference by way of definition:

Both in the French ballet and the English masque, however varied the forms of entertainment might be, there was one constant factor: the *raison d'être* of the whole performance was the arrival of noble personages disguised and masqued to dance a specially prepared dance. They might dance other dances as well, either all together or in groups, but there was one special dance in which they all took part which was the centre of the whole thing, and that dance was known in France as *le grand ballet*, in England as the main or grand masque dance. . . . In France *le grand ballet* was a grand finale. In England it almost always occupied a more or less central position, and was followed by *revels* (i.e. ordinary ballroom dancing between masquers and audience) and by the final dramatic business of speech or song or both, and perhaps a final dance of the masquers, known as the "going off," or "the last dance." [3]

The description, quite adequate for Miss Welsford's purposes, does not entirely represent sixteenth- and seventeenth-century usage. For example, Henry Goldingham's entertainment for Queen Elizabeth at Norwich in 1578 is called "an excellent princely maske," [4] although none of its actors appears to have been noble and it did not lead up to revels, in fact involving no dancing whatsoever. A more puzzling case is to be found in a contemporary description of Ben Jonson's first masque, which was explicitly so called by its author. Sir Dudley Carleton wrote to Sir Ralph Winwood, "At Night we had the Queen's Maske in the Banquetting-House, or rather her Pagent." [5] Miss Welsford, though she cites the description,[6] evidently does not think Carleton's correction of his term especially noteworthy. Carleton, however, must be allowed to be the better judge, and his account of *The Masque*

of Blacknesse is one I shall return to later. Here it will be sufficient to remark that Goldingham's pageant does not satisfy
Miss Welsford's requirements and yet was called a "maske,"
and Jonson's satisfies them perfectly and yet was called a
"Pagent." The definition, then, is adequate if we take it to
express not what the masque was, but what it tended to be.
Certain other characteristics seem to me equally important
for anyone concerned with the idea of the masque which the
seventeenth century inherited, and I shall therefore enlarge
somewhat the limits Miss Welsford has set.

We may begin by looking at a relevant seventeenth-century
passage. The theologian John Smith (d. 1652) compares the
mystical experience of the Biblical prophets with the action
of a court masque:

> The Prophetical scene or Stage upon which all apparitions were
> made to the Prophet, was his Imagination; and that there all
> those things which God would have revealed to him were acted
> over Symbolically, as in a Masque, in which divers persons are
> brought in, amongst which the prophet himself bears a part. And
> therefore he, according to the exigency of this Dramatical appara-
> tus, must, as the other Actors, perform his part.[7]

The Renaissance writer stressed not form, but function and
concept. What characterizes the masque and makes it a valid
metaphor for Smith's purposes is a unique kind of relationship between its action and its audience. Ben Jonson makes
the same point at length in a number of places; but Smith was
not a masque writer and therefore cannot be accused of
special pleading. He is expressing a commonplace, implying
a set of universally accepted assumptions.

The chief characteristic of the masque for Smith is that it
was an occasional production and appealed to its audience in
a very special way. It attempted from the beginning to breach
the barrier between spectators and actors, so that in effect
the viewer became part of the spectacle. The end toward
which the masque moved was to destroy any sense of theater

and to include the whole court in the mimesis — in a sense, what the spectator watched he ultimately became. The most common method of effecting this transformation was to have the production culminate, dramatically and literally, in the revels, the dance between the masquers and members of the audience. But this was by no means the only method, and we find a number of entertainments that approach the same ends by different means, appearing to be masques in structure, though not employing the customary dances and revels. These are not masques *manqués*, but other kinds of the same form, which developed along with the masque Miss Welsford describes and were thought of as analogous entertainments. The value of viewing the masque this way is that we may allow it to be defined not only by what it looked like, but by what, as a form, it was trying to achieve.

Our examination of the form, therefore, must begin with the way the masque related to the event for which it was composed. We have tended to feel — perhaps since the day when Pope purchased his annuity, and certainly since Dr. Johnson composed his definition of *patron* — that writing to order is a violation of the creative spirit. There is no evidence that the Renaissance artist had any such qualms. Ben Jonson's complaints were against his designer, not his employer; and the occasional poem — epithalamion, ode, elegy — was held a perfectly respectable vehicle for saying something worthwhile. Like the occasional poet, the masque writer faced the central problem of making his art relevant to a particular event: giving airy nothing to a local habitation and a name. The masque, of course, was not always poetry and in its early stages often involved only pantomime and dancing. But even those productions designed to be primarily spectacular soon took on the less ephemeral characteristics of dialogue and song; and the devices for masques were in effect being treated as occasional verse long before Jonson declared the independence of his text from its production.[8]

1. THE MASQUE OF PROTEUS

I wish to begin chronologically at the wrong end, with the last Elizabethan masque of which we have a complete text, and treat it as a work embodying all the elements of a tradition that Ben Jonson inherited. *The Mask of Proteus and the Adamantine Rock* is by no means the best of the Tudor entertainments, but it is notable because it is the first one that at all resembles the standard Jacobean masque. We shall see, too, that its similarity to the Jonsonian masque is in some ways more apparent than real; if we can refrain from looking ahead, we shall easily perceive how close it is to its predecessors.

For the season 1594–95, the gentlemen of Gray's Inn had revived the custom of appointing a Lord of Misrule to supervise the revels lasting from Christmas to Shrovetide. He was, a subsequent report tells us, "one Mr. Henry Holmes [Helmes], a Norfolk gentleman, who was thought to be accomplished with all good parts, fit for so great a dignity; and was also a very proper man of personage, and very active in dancing and revelling." [9] Helmes styled himself "Prince of Purpoole," and Gray's Inn became a miniature court during what appear to have been a depressingly sophomoric two months. Part of the prince's time was taken up with an imaginary voyage to visit "the great and mighty emperor of all Russia," one "Theodore Evanwich." [10] It was to represent the triumphant return from this journey that a colleague, Francis Davison, composed *The Mask of Proteus and the Adamantine Rock*, which also served to conclude Helmes's reign.

The masque was performed at court by the gentlemen of Gray's Inn at Shrovetide (March 3 or 4), 1595. The queen was evidently highly pleased with it.[11] The text as we have it gives very little information about the production, but it does not appear to have been especially spectacular. When Elizabeth and her court entered the Banqueting House at Whitehall, what they saw was a simple scaffold stage at one end, with the adamantine rock of the title as a prominent fixture. The stage had no curtain and no proscenium arch, and there is no reason to assume that the rock, from which the masquers issued forth, was anything more elaborate than a painted canvas flat large enough to conceal eight people.

Rudimentary as this staging seems, it nevertheless represents a departure from the traditional method. Normally, the action of the Tudor masque took place in the center of the hall and was surrounded by the audience. Sometimes there was no stage at all, but only various properties — a rock, a tree, a bower — distributed about the floor. More often, a series of moveable stages, pageant cars, presented the action. Both properties and pageants were removed before the beginning of the dancing that generally concluded these entertainments. *The Mask of Proteus*, with its fixed stage and its unified setting, is the first English masque to conceive, in however small a way, of the masquing hall as a theater. This is an innovation with which Inigo Jones is usually credited,[12] but he was not the first to think of it. He was the first to realize that it was an improvement and to exploit its possibilities. What was theatrically new about *The Masque of Blacknesse* in 1605 was its sophistication of an old device, the complexity achieved with such a setting and the mechanical development of such a stage.

To the Elizabethans, Proteus was a ubiquitous figure, a symbol of life in the sublunary world. He was the mythological representative of two central themes of the literature of the age: the dangers of inconstancy and the deceptiveness of appearances. But his particular significance for the writer of

masques stems from a more ancient tradition and is explained
by Lucian in his dialogue, "Of Pantomime":

If I am not mistaken, the Egyptian Proteus of ancient legend
is no other than a dancer whose mimetic skill enables him to
adapt himself to every character: in the activity of his movements,
he is liquid as water, rapid as fire; he is the raging lion, the sav-
age panther, the trembling bough; he is what he will. The legend
takes these data, and gives them a supernatural turn, — for
mimicry substituting metamorphosis. Our modern pantomimes
have the same gift, and Proteus himself sometimes appears as
the subject of their rapid transformations.[13]

He is, in a sense, the spirit of the masque, the embodiment
of the idea of disguising. Yet, to the Elizabethan, he is also
the great enemy Mutability, threatening the establishment of
order and denying the value of permanence. Davison therefore makes Proteus both the center of his masque world and
its archvillain. The work is built around him, but its action
is his defeat and submission.

The masque opens unceremoniously enough with the entrance of the four characters with speaking roles: first Proteus, the villain, and his adversary, an Esquire of the Prince
of Purpoole; then, as an admiring audience for their debate,
Thamesis, the river Thames, and Amphitrite, goddess of the
sea. The Esquire is attended by a Tartar page, Proteus by two
tritons, and the goddesses by two sea nymphs; the comparative simplicity of the stage and its setting is compensated by
the exotic appearance of nine masquers in the traditionally
fantastic costumes of court revels. The nymphs and tritons
are musicians and open the masque with a song.[14] Their
hymn in praise of Neptune is brief and poetically the best
part of the work:

> Of Neptunes Empyre let us sing,
> At whose command the waves obay:
> To whom the Rivers tribute pay,
> Downe the high mountaines sliding.

To whom the skaly Nation yeelds
Homage for the Cristall fields
   Wherein they dwell;
And every Sea-god paies a Jem,
Yeerely out of his watry Cell,
To decke great Neptunes Diadem.

The Trytons dauncing in a ring,
Before his Pallace gates, doo make
The water with their Ecchoes quake,
Like the great Thunder sounding:
The Sea-Nymphes chaunt their Accents shrill,
And the Syrens taught to kill
   With their sweet voyce;
Make ev'ry ecchoing Rocke reply
Unto their gentle murmuring noyse,
The prayse of Neptunes Empery.

The praise of a sovereign is germane to the masque form, and the tendency to confuse the monarch of the sea with the ruler of the queen's navy was common even in Elizabethan times. Nevertheless, we should note the vitality with which the conventional hymn has been treated, the richness and particularity of the images, and the sureness of the verse. The song is an apt and striking beginning, the work of a fully accomplished poet. Seven years later, when Davison included the poem in his *Poetical Rhapsody*, he ascribed it to one of the best English songwriters, his fellow Grayan, Thomas Campion.[15]

Though Davison's ensuing speeches cannot pretend to the quality of Campion's verse, they testify to a genuine concern for the logical and dramatic coherence of the masque. The legal mind at play works in amusingly literalistic ways. The Esquire's response to the opening song is to wonder at its being produced by minions of Proteus; for philosophers hold that sea creatures have no interest in music and, indeed, may very possibly be deaf. To this Aristotelian hypothesis Proteus returns a curt Baconian reply, suggesting that philosophers try living under water before they theorize about it and citing as a piece of empirical evidence the experience of the dolphin charmed by Arion's music.

This exchange apparently is Davison's gesture to the frivolity of the occasion: the dialogue at once settles down to the serious business of explaining how these creatures of the sea and their great rock happen to be at Whitehall. Davison recognized that the function of his text was to provide a suitable device for the entry of the masquers, and a suitable fiction for honoring the queen. So dialogue is subordinated to dance, the demands of drama to those of the occasion. The explanations are accomplished in what Amphitrite calls "fair set Speeches" (line 66) [16] — they are also very long set speeches — which make only the merest pretense of being dramatic.

The Esquire tells how his master, the Prince of Purpoole, during his recent travels, had managed to capture Proteus. The sea god had resorted to all his usual transformations to regain his liberty, but the prince had held fast until an adequate ransom was offered. Proteus had promised to bring the "Adamantine Rock, the Sea's true Star," which would give its possessor control of "the wild Empire of the Ocean," to whatever place the prince wished, but added the condition,

> Which, as he thought, would no way be perform'd;
> That first the Prince should bring him to a power,
> Which in attractive Vertue should surpass
> The wondrous force of his Iron-drawing Rocks.
>
> (181–184)

The prince agreed and further consented to being shut up in the rock with seven of his knights as hostages. The rock and Proteus are now at the appointed place for the trial, the palace at Whitehall.

The sea god states his case. He rests secure in the strength of his giant lodestone:

> What needeth words, when great effects proclaim

The' attractive virtue of th'Adamantine rocks?
Which forceth iron, which all things else commands?
(196–198)

But the Esquire is unmoved:

Calm awhile your overweening vaunts;
Prepare belief, and do but use your eyes,
(219–220)

he sneers, and directs Proteus' attention outward, beyond the limits of the stage and the fictive world, toward their royal spectator. He invokes Elizabeth, more powerful than the lodestone, "true Adamant of hearts." It is she who is (as Hamlet will say at a more famous court entertainment) "metal more attractive."

Initially, the distinction being presented is a simple one between the physical and the moral: the Esquire is able to demonstrate the superiority of spiritual qualities over the material forces represented by Proteus. But the sea god's defeat involves a more subtle distinction as well. He is a literalist; his faith is founded on a rock, his vision bounded by the properties of his world, which are after all only stage properties. He is helpless before a figure who can step outside that world and who can see the properties of the rock as metaphorical rather than physical — a figure, in short, who knows that he is an actor in a masque and is conscious of the presence and significance of the audience.

This does seem to be taking unfair advantage of Proteus, and, indeed, only the villain of a masque can be vanquished in so unsporting a manner. It is the function of the form to acknowledge explicitly the audience for whom it is created; for a character not to know that such an audience exists must be interpreted as a kind of moral blindness, an inability to see the true nature of his world. It is dramatic irony that defeats Proteus. The hero possesses knowledge of which the villain can hardly conceive, and it is a kind of knowledge peculiar to the heroes of masques. Davison is giving dramatic expression to that quality which John Smith found central to the form, the identification of masquers and spectators; the villain alone is limited by the fiction, the dramatic illusion. The hero moves beyond it at will and is aware of his place in a larger world. What he knows is what the audience knows.

This distinction, present here in a most elementary form, is basic to every court masque, and we shall find it elaborated and deepened as we consider more complex and artful examples of the genre. For masques have a very special way of disposing of their villains, who differ from the heroes in more than ethical respects. In Jacobean times, the two figures had even come to inhabit different worlds — for the villain, the antimasque, for the hero, the masque. To Ben Jonson, this was already a convention of the form and served him as one of many tools for establishing more profound distinctions of sensibility and morality. Thus, the characters in Jonsonian antimasques, played by professional actors, are nearly always unaware that there are spectators;[17] but his masquers, court ladies and gentlemen, regularly conclude their revels by joining the spectators in a dance.

Proteus is, then, an embryonic antimasque character. The Esquire is the spokesman of the masque and embodies a special kind of awareness. This sort of artistic self-consciousness, whereby the virtue or power of a figure is dependent on his ability not to take himself or his world literally, is rare outside the masque. But there are analogues; Prospero is an obvious one. Similarly, Spenser's Sir Guyon is reminded by his palmer that his enemies are abstractions and it is pointless for him to attempt to kill them — reminded, that is, that he is a character in an allegory, not a romance.[18] To a villain, such awareness becomes especially valuable. Spenser's Amoret is kidnapped by a magician who knows how to use conventions for his own ends:

> For that same vile Enchantour *Busyran,*
> The very selfe same day that she was wedded . . .

Brought in that mask of love which late was showen:
And there the Ladie ill of friends bestedded,
By way of sport, as oft in maskes is knowen,
Conveyed quite away to living wight unknowen.

(IV.i.3)

Middleton's machiavel, De Flores, has an even more complex kind of knowledge. He hides a sword on stage in preparation for committing a murder during the interval between acts — a time that, as far as the other characters are concerned, does not exist. Hero or villain, the figure who is capable of stepping outside or violating the conventions of his form is by nature invincible; and that figure in Davison's masque is the Esquire.

In part, of course, Proteus loses in the trial through a lawyer's trick, a play on words. But in the world of the masque, the trope also expresses a literal truth; the metaphorical "Adamant of hearts," the queen's "attractive vertue," has the same power as the lodestone. The argument against the sea god, then, is formulated with a firm sense of fact and all the acumen of a gentleman of Gray's Inn:

> Proteus, stout Iron-Homager of your rock,
> Impresa of force, and Instruments of Wars,
> Hath praise indeed; yet place your Praises right;
> For force to will, and wars to peace do yield.
> But that I'll give you. This I wou'd fain know,
> What can your iron do without arms of men?
> And arms of men from hearts of men do move:
> The hearts of men, that's it thence motion springs.
> Lo Proteus then, the attractive Rock of hearts . . .
> Your rock claims kindred of the Polar star,
> Because it draws the needle to the North;
> Yet even that star gives place to Cynthia's rays
> Whose drawing virtues govern and direct
> The flots and re-flots of the Ocean . . .
> What excellencies are there in this frame,
> Of all things which her Vertue doth not draw?
> **Fish-herd divine, congratulate yourself,**

> Your eyes have won more than your state hath lost;
> Yield Victory, and Liberty, and Thanks.   (229–281)

The villain concedes, blessing "that Prince that forc'd me see this Grace" and adding his praises to the occasion. Then, fulfilling his bargain, he strikes the rock and calls forth the hostage masquers, the prince and his seven knights.

So the hero triumphs and the villain repents. But not as in a drama, for the confutation of Proteus takes place essentially before the action even begins. The *coup de grâce* comes as the answer to an extended riddle ("What figure will satisfy the following requirements?") rather than as the culmination of a series of related events. Dialogue has a special function here. It is being used not, as in a play, to convey the action and bring about its resolution, but instead to *delay* the resolution, which is inherent, like the answer to a riddle, in the very statement of the problem. No process is involved; there is no dialectic between a riddle and its answer.

Drama, therefore, is held to a minimum after the opening exchange: we note, for example, that the Esquire describes what Proteus has done, though the latter is on stage and might just as well tell us in his own words. We may, of course, wish to charge Davison with ineptitude, but even Jonson is careful to keep the figures of his masques from turning into characters suitable for a play. And finally, when the only thing in the piece that may be described as action occurs, it significantly involves no dialogue:

Hereat Proteus, Amphitrite and Thamesis, with their Attendants, the Nymphs and Tritons, went unto the Rock, and then the Prince and the seven Knights issued forth of the Rock, in a very stately Mask, very richly attired, and gallantly provided of all things meet for the performance of so great an Enterprize. They come forth of the Rock in Couples, and before every Couple come two Pigmies with Torches. [Then they dance] . . . After which they took unto them Ladies; and with them they danced . . . after the end whereof the Pigmies brought eight Escutcheons,

with the Maskers Devices thereupon, and delivered them to the
Esquire, who offered them to Her Majesty; which being done,
they took their Order again, and with a new Strain, went all into
the Rock; at which time there was sung another new Hymn
within the Rock.   (295ff)

The masque's conclusion is provided by dance and music.
Indeed, as we shall see, it is characteristic of the kind of action
masques present that it can take place only in a world purged
of drama, of conflict. Even in *Proteus*, the syllogism that has
defeated the villain is clearly implicit in the agreement he
has made with the prince: the very threat of evil implies its
destruction in this world, and both the threat and the triumph over it belong to the exposition. What the masque presents is not the achievement of that triumph, but a celebration of it.

I have said that the examination of any court masque ought
to begin with the way it deals with the occasion for which it
was composed. Certain later masques — notably Jonson's —
claim for themselves the enduring virtues of poetry as well as
the ephemeral ones of the production. *Proteus* claims only
the latter, and Davison presumably considered Campion's
opening song alone to be worthy of publication. The remaining speeches he preserved in a very careful and beautiful
manuscript, which seems to be in his own hand.[19] It provides
the best text we have of the piece (though curiously omitting
the hymn to Neptune) and may suggest that the author
wished his work to endure not for the sake of art or the attention of a literary audience, but as a memento of an event important primarily to himself and other gentlemen of Gray's
Inn. He would perhaps have considered it fitting that the
manuscript should have passed into the hands of John Stow,
the antiquary, whose interest would not have been in the
quality of its verse. When the masque was finally printed in
1688, it formed only a small part of an account of the revels

of 1594–95, the season when the Grayans had provided so much of the royal entertainment. So the emphasis of both versions of *Proteus* that have come down to us is on the occasion for which it was produced.

The center of that occasion was Queen Elizabeth. Obviously her actual presence is a prerequisite of the production: on the most superficial level, because it is conceived as a compliment to her and would make no sense if applied to anyone else; on the fictive level, because her "attractive vertue" is necessary to effect the triumph of the prince over Proteus. Her role emphasizes again the nondramatic nature of the form, for through her the masque moves toward its one significant action — the release of the dancers — and it is action without a hint of drama. The queen makes this central event possible, turning the dialogue to dance, the speeches to their traditional conclusion in the revels — in effect, making the masque a masque. In the deepest sense, then, the physical presence of Elizabeth gives *Proteus* its meaning.

Undoubtedly Davison's use of the queen is somewhat perfunctory; she is required only to be a spectator. But in more complex masques the sovereign stays in the center of the masque universe, and the nature of the action involved is correspondingly more complex. If we trace the idea of the monarch-as-actor back through the Elizabethan and Tudor disguisings, we shall see first that Davison's version is perfunctory not because it is archaic, but because it is essentially a simplification of a highly developed convention; and more generally, we shall see something of the variety and depth of the tradition.

2. THE MONARCH AS MASQUER

The problem of incorporating the monarch into the masque was considerably simplified if he was himself one of the masquers, if he took part literally as well as figuratively. This Queen Elizabeth did only rarely, and her successor, never. Henry VIII, on the other hand, loved to disguise himself. Though records of court entertainments from the earlier reigns are scanty, we do find several productions in which parts were played by the king. In a very early example, at Christmas 1377 a group of mummers appeared before the court and the young prince who was to be Richard II, and offered to play dice with them. The dice were "subtilly made so that when the prince shold cast he shold winne": "the said players and mummers set before the prince three jewels each after other: and first a balle of gould, then a Cupp of Gould, then a gould ring the which the said prince wonne at three castes as before it was appointed." [20] There is kind of rudimentary drama here: the fiction is that a game of chance is taking place, and the work thus contains adversaries and a central action. But chance has been defeated — the dice are loaded, and the prince always wins. The masquers implicitly characterize Richard in the same terms Mark Antony was to use of a luckier monarch: "The very dice obey him" and, literally for Richard, as figuratively for Octavius, "The odds is gone." The sovereign wins, the masque says, because it is his nature to win; and this concept of the nature of the monarch is, in one form or another, at the root of every court masque.

In a more usual kind of disguising, the sovereign is presented with gifts by symbolic figures, often representing deities. I have already mentioned Goldingham's "excellent princely maske," presented before Elizabeth in 1578, in which a procession of gods and goddesses recited verses and offered presents. There was no dancing and not even the most perfunctory sort of drama: the sole function of the piece was in the giving of the gifts. Now this is also the purpose behind Richard II's disguising. What has been eliminated is the game of chance, that is, the monarch no longer wins the gifts, he now *deserves* them. The distinction is, of course, only illusory, since Richard always won. And if we go a step further and say that, whatever a writer might make of his masque, its function on the most simple level was always to honor the monarch, we shall perceive an essential relationship between such disparate pieces as Goldingham's masque and Davison's *Proteus*.

When the masque was conceived in more dramatic terms, the sovereign's position became more complex. Early in the fifteenth century, John Lydgate wrote the speeches for a group of mummings, one of which is relevant to our purpose. It was presented before Henry VI at Hertford Castle, around 1430, and is described in the manuscript as "a disguysing of the Rude upplandisshe people compleyning in hir wyves with the boystous aunswere of hir wyves." [21] Here a master of ceremonies leads in the mummers and presents each of the husbands in turn, listing their complaints. The wives then speak for themselves, offering a defense of their behavior — and citing, by the way, the example of "the worthy wyff of Bathe" (line 168). Finally, the king is asked to determine who is in the right. The text informs us that "the kyng yivethe ther upon sentence and Jugement" (line 215); but, as one might expect, he declines to settle so nice a question. The speech itself is delivered again by the master of ceremonies, though in King Henry's name. The monarch, then, has a place in the dramatic stucture of Lydgate's mumming: the players present a problem that it is Henry's function to resolve.

We might note, along with this literal use of the royal presence, that the fiction of the masque also uses the actual setting and situation in which the performance takes place. Not that we are to think of the piece as realistic; "rude upplandisshe people" would not, presumably, quote Chaucer to prove a point. But we are not transported to a mythical landscape, and the king is not allegorized: he stands only for himself. The masque is the dramatization of an old joke, and everything is done to keep it as fresh and close to the contemporary world as possible. To the audience, the most remarkable part of the entertainment may well have been the fact that the wives answered for themselves. In a mumming the actors were usually, though not necessarily, expected to be mum, as were Prince Richard's dicers and the husbands here. Evidently it was an innovation for Lydgate to have provided a text for what was basically pantomime. So this Hertford entertainment combines the conventional elements of a disguising before the sovereign with a more complex idea of drama. It is an idea that depends heavily on the facts of the production, the occasion, and the setting, and includes the king within the dramatic framework.

We have remarked that Henry does not actually decide the issue of the mumming. We accept the judgment offered by the master of ceremonies as coming from the king because the king has been defined in the piece as that figure whose function it is to arbitrate and thereby to maintain the dramatic illusion. In a more complex but perfectly analogous way, Elizabeth is used to establish the meaning of Davison's *Proteus*. The next step for Lydgate would logically have been to give the king a part to speak, though the impossibility of doing so in 1430 is obvious: there was as yet in England no tradition for the king to be the chief masquer, and one could not very well reduce him to the level of a common mummer. Even two centuries later, courtly masquers rarely had speaking parts. Nevertheless, the step was taken by an Elizabethan writer whose characteristic quality was that he examined and altered whatever convention he used. Sidney's *The Lady of May* is unquestionably the finest of the pre-Jacobean entertainments, and in Sidney's masque, Queen Elizabeth not only spoke to settle a dramatic contention, but was apparently required to devise her own part. She gave her decision on the spot in a speech that, whether or not it was prepared, was certainly not provided by Sidney.

Few accounts of fifteenth-century court productions remain to us, but it is clear that by the last years of the reign of Henry VII, music and dancing had become a staple element of a form that was beginning to show real consistency. Music and dancing, in fact, often excluded dialogue entirely; masquers tended to be silent, and the significance of the work began to be carried by its often elaborate choreography and symbolic scenic effects. At the same time, the sovereign had become a more integral part of the masque than ever before by taking on the role of the chief masquer. Clearly a different kind of entertainment from Lydgate's is involved here. Unless we begin to think of the masque as a game, rather than as a show, the part of masquer will be a difficult one in which to imagine the king, since he had effectively ceased to be part of the audience. The writer's problem now becomes how to create a masque figure that the king can portray or, conversely, how to create a figure that will serve as an adequate representation of the monarch beneath the mask.

One early way of dealing with the problem is exemplified in a masque prepared by William Newark, Master of the Chapel, to celebrate the wedding of Henry VII's son Prince Arthur and Katherine of Aragon in 1501. "When the King and the Queen had taken their noble seates under their Clothes of estate," the account informs us, "began and Entered this most goodly and pleasant disguising convayed and shewed in pageantes proper and subtile." [22] These were drawn into the hall on wheels and served as the setting for a medieval allegory. The first pageant was a castle with eight "goodly and fresh ladyes looking out of the windowes" and in the four turrets "fowre Children singing most sweetly and hermoniously in all the Comming the length of the hall till they came before the Kinges majestie."

Next came a pageant resembling a ship, which stopped beside the castle. At this point there was some dialogue, for "the masters of the Shippe and their Company in their counteynaunces speaches and demeanor used and behaved them selves after the manner and guise of Mariners." Even more important, we learn that "in the . . . shippe there was a goodly and faire ladye in her apparell like unto the Princesse of Spaine" — that is, like the bride, Katherine of Aragon. "Out and from the said shippe descended downe by a ladder two well beseene and goodly persons calling them selves hope and desire"; they present themselves to the ladies of the castle as ambassadors from the Knights of the Mount of Love, "making great instance in the behalfe of the said Knightes" and acting "as wooers and breakers of the maters of love betweene the Knightes and Ladyes." But the ladies are unmoved: they "gave their small aunsweare of utterly refuse and knowledge of any such Company or that they were ever minded to the accomplishment of any such request and plainely denyed their purpose and desire."

The ambassadors threaten retaliation. At once "came in the third Pageant in likenes of a great hill or mountaine in whom there was inclosed viii goodly Knightes . . . naming them selves the Knightes of the mount of love." This too was drawn up before the king and queen, "and then these two Ambassadors departed to the Knightes . . . shewing the disdaine and refusall with the whole circumstance of the same." The knights "hastely spedd them to the . . . Castle which they forthwith assaulted." The ladies yield and descend, "being right freshly disguised . . . fower of them after the English fashion and the other ffour after the manner of Spaine" and, to conclude the action, "daunced together divers and many goodly daunces."

As an evening's diversion, this elaborate piece must have served admirably. An audience of 1501 would not have been startled to find castles and mountains as mobile as ships and would in any case have enjoyed the splendor of the production and the symbolism of the pageants. The allegory is simple and appropriate to a royal wedding. The Princess of Aragon has come with Hope and Desire from the Mount of Love; she is an envoy of Venus or may represent the goddess herself. With this figure presiding from the deck of her ship, the eight knights win the ungracious ladies of England and Spain over to the cause of Love. Now the reader may have noticed one awkward detail in the story. Katherine has come to England as a bride, but, alone of the disguisers, the "faire ladye in her apparell like unto the Princesse of Spaine" is left without a partner. The knights dance off with their ladies, but the disguising provides no Mars, nor even the brief consolation of a Tannhäuser for the queen of this Venusberg. Her apparent abandonment would not have disturbed a contemporary spectator, who was probably more interested in the figure as a symbol of love than in the strict working out of an allegory. For us, the fact that the symbol does not quite fit the reality need be no more than a reminder that there is nothing especially modern about the gap between art and life. The problem of bringing them into coincidence can become peculiarly pressing in the art form we are considering.

Obviously the allegorical disguising was the most important part of this evening in 1501. Nevertheless, with the conclusion of the disguising, the entertainment was not yet over. The real Katherine does have her moment on the dancing floor, but not until all traces of what, after all, has been a representation of herself have disappeared. The account continues, "in the tyme of their [the eight knights' and ladies'] dauncing the three Pageantes the Castle the shippe and the

mountain removed and departed the same wise the disguisers
. . . as well the Knightes as the Ladyes after certaine leasure
of their solace and disport avoyded and evanished out of
their sight and presence." Only when the masquers and
pageants have left the hall do the lords and ladies of the court
descend and dance themselves. They too seem part of the
masque, for their dances have clearly been carefully prepared:

And then came downe the Lord Prince and the Ladye Cecill and
daunced two baas daunces and departed up again the Lord Prince
to the King and the Ladye Cecill to the Queene eftsoones the
Ladye Princesse and one of her ladyes with her in apparell after
the Spanish guise came downe there dauncing other two baas
daunces and departed againe bothe up to the Queene. Third and
last came downe the Duke of Yorke having with him the Ladye
Margret his sister in his hand and daunced two baas daunces and
afterwards he perceiving him selfe to be accombred with his
Clothes sodainly cast of his gowne and daunced in his Jackett
with the said Ladye Margarett in so goodly and pleasant maner
that it was to the Kinge and Queen right great and singular
pleasure and so departed againe the Duke to the Kinge and the
Ladye to the Queene. Thus this disguising royall thus ended.

All the elements of the mature Tudor disguising are here,
though they have not quite come together yet. The occasional
nature of the work is all that recalls Lydgate's mumming.
Newark's masque looks very different: we note the use of
symbolic pageants, the emphasis on allegory, music, and
dance rather than dialogue to carry the meaning, and especially the concluding dances by those who have been spectators. On the other hand, no unifying idea is in evidence.
The work does not prepare in any logical way for the descent
of the courtiers, and the lack of connection between the disguising and the dances which (it was evidently felt) had to
close the entertainment is exemplified in the way the two sections are strictly separated. Disguisers and courtiers could
not be on the floor at the same time.

The "monarch" in this work (the person honored) is

Katherine of Aragon. She does not take part in the disguising itself, but she is the central figure. In a sense she watches
herself; she is both actor and spectator, and to a certain extent the boundary between stage and audience has been removed. We might take as analogues any of the royal entries of
the period in which, as the monarch rode through the streets
of a town, he saw tableaux representing his own triumphs
or allegories dedicated to his greatness. In these and in the
wedding masque, the monarch has not yet stepped on the
stage, but neither is he wholly off it.

It took a somewhat less literalistic artist than William
Newark to decide that, in a disguising, the reality and the
symbol might be allowed to exist simultaneously: the courtiers might dance with the figures of fiction; the hall at West-
minster might be both the English court and an allegorical
landscape; and most significant, the actual monarch might
merge with the masquer who represented him. The means
toward achieving this unification of the form seem in large
measure to have been provided by that same Duke of York
who had "cast of his gowne and daunced in his Jackett . . .
in so goodly and pleasant maner" at his brother's wedding
masque, Katherine's second husband, Henry VIII. The artists
whose names we find most frequently associated with the
entertainments of the first fifteen years of the new reign are
William Cornysshe, the Master of the Chapel after Newark's
death in 1509, and Richard Gibson.

Yet even under what seem to have been ideal conditions,
the development of the form was a slow one. In fact, there
exist no pre-Elizabethan masques that wholly embody the
sort of unity I have been describing, though they are all
clearly moving toward it. We can perceive a growing idea of
form in the series of pageants Cornysshe and Gibson prepared
for King Henry. Early in the reign, the entertainment begins
to include revels, which involve the breakdown of the barrier
between stage and spectators. In 1512, for the first time in an

English masque, the masquers took their partners from among the ladies of the court. The contemporary account given by Edward Halle makes clear the provenance of the idea and also how great a departure it was from traditional usage:

On the daie of the Epiphanie at night, the kyng with a.xi. other wer disguised, after the maner of Italie, called a maske, a thyng not seen afore in Englande . . . after the banket doen, these Maskers came in . . . and desired the ladies to daunce, some were content, and some that knewe the fashion of it refused, because it was not a thyng commonly seen. And after thei daunced and commoned together, as the fashion of the Maskes is, thei toke their leave and departed, and so did the Quene, and all the ladies.[23]

As Paul Reyher shows, it was the revels that had not been "seen afore" and that resembled the licentious behavior of contemporary Italian masques;[24] this is the "fashion" that made some of the ladies refuse. But no one could refuse for long, knowing that beneath the disguise danced the king. From this time on, the revels gradually became an essential part of one kind of court masque, and it provided the means by which the spectators were integral to the entertainment they watched. When the monarch has moved into the masque world, the court is obliged to follow.

The entertainment of 1512 as Halle describes it is not, of course, a masque of the type we are considering. It is only revels and makes no attempt to provide dramatic justification for the entry of the masquers. The work gains its effect from the surprise of the dancers' sudden appearance, their rich and exotic costumes ("thei were appareled in garmentes long and brode, wrought all with gold, with visers and cappes of gold, and . . . came in, with six gentlemen disguised in silke bearyng staffe torches" [25]), and in general the strangeness of the whole idea. But the device of the revels could now be applied to more complex court entertainments. This was not done immediately, and it is not until much later that the revels become the only way to conclude a masque. Still, the precedent has been set; and the ease with which Cornysshe and Gibson were able to use members of the court in their productions is evidence that the new fashion was rapidly accepted as a conventional element of the form. At first, in fact, we find not the simple joining of hands between the two worlds that the revels represent, but a veritable exodus of courtiers into the world of the masque.

On Epiphany of the next year, 1513, for example, there was a pageant called *The Riche Mount*, which presented a golden mountain with broom plants and "riche flowers of silke" (red and white roses?) growing on it. This signified "Plantagenet" and bears witness to the perennial ingenuity of the literate Englishman, who even today would have no difficulty with a crossword hint like "Royalty overgrown with French broom?" Atop the mountain "stode a goodly Bekon geving light," writes the observant Halle; "rounde about the Bekon sat the king and five other." These six, Henry and his lords, descended and danced; then the mount opened and six ladies appeared who danced first by themselves and then with the six men. The ladies re-entered the pageant, the five lords presumably making their own way out of the hall, while the King "shifted hym [changed from his costume] and came to the Quene, and sat at the banquet." [26]

This work does not conclude with revels; and Henry's return to the table without his disguise is less the entrance of a masque figure into the world of the spectators than a simple acknowledgment that the chief dancer is also the chief courtier. But, equally clearly, the pageant no longer provides the kind of entertainment with which William Newark had honored Katherine's wedding twelve years earlier. The direction Cornysshe and Gibson have taken is toward narrowing and intensifying the masque: the pageant of 1501 is primarily a show and could have been presented before any spectator

whether he was a member of the court or not. It tells an allegorical story and relies for its effect mainly on the elaborateness of its production and only secondarily on the special fact
that it is about the princess who is watching it. *The Riche
Mount* has no plot at all, and it depends on its production in
the same ways as the earlier disguising — but not entirely. For
now the primary element of the masque is the relationship
it sets up between the noble dancers and the disguises they
wear, between the allegory of the mount and the fact that it
really does contain the king.

The symbolic pageants during Henry's reign soon became
more than tableaux. After 1515 they regularly (though not
always) included speeches — at first only by way of prologue,
but soon to convey part of the action. They always concluded
with a dance by a number of courtiers headed by the king and
sometimes with revels. From such descriptions as Halle's we
gather that they were lavishly produced and that Cornysshe's
music played an increasingly great role in their success. When
there was dialogue (especially after Cornysshe's death in
1524, when William Crane became Master of the Chapel), it
was apparently a significant, if small, element in the masque.
And we do find under Crane the beginnings of an attempt to
integrate the pageant with the now indispensable court
dances. This unifying movement is the most important part
of the development we have been considering. It is exemplified in one of the most ambitious of King Henry's entertainments, the Greenwich masque *Riches and Love*, devised by
Crane to be shown during a visit of French ambassadors and
presented on May 6, 1527.

After an oration about the newly established friendship
between France and England, eight children of the chapel,
singing, entered at either side of the hall, bringing with them
two richly costumed figures. These two then debated whether
riches or love were better. Unable to agree, each summoned
three knights, who fought at barriers across a golden bar that

suddenly dropped from an arch in the center of the hall. Again neither side won, and the knights withdrew. "Then," recounts Halle, "came in an olde man with a silver berd, and he concluded that love and riches, both be necessarie for princes (that is to saie) by love to be obeied and served, and with riches to rewarde his lovers and frendes, and with this conclusion the dialogue ended." [27]

Immediately the masquing began. "Then at the nether ende, by lettyng doune of a courtaine, apered a goodly mount" with a fortress; the mount was studded with rubies and other precious stones, and planted with roses and pomegranates. On it were eight lords gorgeously dressed, who at once descended, took partners from the audience, and danced. "Then out of a cave issued out the ladie Mary doughter to the kyng and with her seven ladies," richly dressed "after the romayne fashion," who danced with the eight lords of the mount; "and as thei daunced, sodenly entred six personages," in silver and black; "there garments were long after the fashion of Iseland," and they wore "visers with sylver berdes, so that they were not knowne." They too took partners from the audience and "daunced lustly about the place." Then suddenly the king, who had secretly left the hall, entered with seven lords, masked "after the Venicians fashion," their faces vizarded with beards of gold. "Then with minstrelsie these viii . . . daunced long with the ladies, and when they had daunced there fyll, then the quene plucked of the kynges visar, and so did the Ladies the visars of the other Lords, and then all were knowen." [28]

Each of the elements is clearly defined here: the dialogue, with its interlude of the barriers, followed by the masque dances and revels. Halle has evidently missed a good deal in the masquing section. From his description we derive little sense of what must have been a kind of ballet on the theme of the dialogue, for the pageant-mountain is covered with jewels, roses, and pomegranates, obvious symbols of riches

and love.[29] In the absence of a text or a more detailed summary, any consideration of the work must remain fairly
general. Nevertheless, we can see that its two main sections,
dialogue and masquing, are connected both symbolically
and, in a rudimentary way, dramatically; they are not, that
is, discrete treatments of the same theme. The debate has
ended in a resolution of the apparent antithesis of riches and
love. At once a pageant enters displaying symbols of this unification and bearing masked dancers. It is impossible to determine at this distance the whole meaning — what the figures
represented, particularly those mysterious Icelanders — but
it is evident at least that no conflict is being represented in
the dances, which present a choreographic version of the
harmony achieved by the dialogue.

We shall readily perceive what an advance this is over
earlier disguisings if we consider the sort of unity found in
The Riche Mount of 1513 and the pageants that followed
soon after. For example, the Greenwich entertainment of
1515 ("Pavyllyon un the Plas Parlos") was in pantomime,
but evidently this would not adequately bear the weight of
the meaning, so we find that "Mr. Kornysshe, Mr. Krane, Mr.
Harry . . . first declared the intent of the pageant by process
of speech." [30] The Eltham barriers of the next year is an
episodic work in which three strange knights challenge and
battle the defenders of a castle for no apparent reason. When
the barriers are over and the attackers have been driven off,
the lords and ladies of the castle emerge and dance. There are
occasional explanatory "spechys after the devys of Mr. Kornyche." [31] In these entertainments, the solutions to the problem of formal coherence are not essentially different from
Lydgate's use of a narrator, eighty-five years earlier, to inter-
pret the action of his mummers.

In Davison's *Proteus*, the basic function of the dialogue
was to provide a reason for the entry of the masquers; the
debate between Proteus and the Esquire both explained the

masquing and was dramatically integral to it. The value of this sort of dramatic unity in the masque seems to have been felt first by Crane. Earlier productions tended to have only the unity of a pageant, symbolic and thematic. But *Riches and Love* recognizes other requirements: the debate offers a reason for the barriers it includes and, in the resolving of its conflict, explains and makes possible the symbolic dances. So the revels begin, superseding dialogue and action and embodying that final harmony which the drama has achieved. The masquing section extends this harmony out beyond the confines of dramatic fiction into the world of the audience and the realities of the court. As soon as the knights descend from their pageant, it is apparent that there is no barrier between masquer and spectator. The carefully organized series of dances gradually involves more and more of the court and culminates in the final merging of symbol and reality, the removal of the masks so that "all were knowen" and the revelation that the chief masquer is also the king. The debate had been a didactic statement about the nature of kingship and the relation of the monarch to his court. To a contemporary audience, the dances must have seemed a realization of that abstract lesson. With the king's unmasking, the illusion was at last firmly established in the actual world of royal protocol, and the admiration of spectator for dancer turned necessarily to the homage of subject for sovereign.

I would take this masque of Crane's to represent the mature Tudor disguising. Records are lacking from the later years of Henry's reign, but, judging from the entertainments provided for his son and eldest daughter, the masque tended to show a simplification of the elements of *Riches and Love* rather than any real advance in the form. Edward VI himself recorded in his diary a description of the disguising for Epiphany of 1552, which is obviously in some way germane to the dialogue of 1527.

The same night was first a play, after a talk between one that was called Riches, and th'other Youth, wither of them was bettir. After some prety reasoning there came in six champions, of either side . . . [here he names the twelve courtiers who took part.] Al thes fought tow to tow at barrieres in the hall. Then cam in tow apparelled like almaines, Th'erle of Ormonde and Jacques Granado. And tow cam in like friers, but the almaines wold not suffer them to pase til they had fought. The friers were Mr Drury and Thomas Cobham. After this followed tow maskes on of men another of women. Then a banket of 120 dishes. This was th'end of Christmas.[32]

It has been argued that this masque and *Riches and Love* were both written by John Heywood,[33] but it is hardly necessary to postulate a single author to account for the similarity between the two works. The form dialogue-barriers-masquing had been used before 1527 and was doubtless not unusual afterwards; anybody who had been at court for a few Christmases might have seen such a show — and could, in any case, have read the very descriptions I have cited from Halle's chronicle, either in manuscript or in the editions of 1548 or 1550. Furthermore, we might wonder how similar the two works actually are. For while the dialogue of 1552 is certainly relevant to the fifteen-year-old king, *Riches and Youth* hardly seems to offer the same sort of antithesis as *Riches and Love.* Insofar as both deal with qualities possessed by the monarch, they are alike; but the "prety reasoning" in each would have been totally different, and we may doubt whether the works had much more than the basic, and by now conventional, elements in common. The point is that during the Tudor period there was an established form and tradition for the masque. If King Edward was not, like his father, the chief masquer, nevertheless it is clear from his description that a great part of his interest in this particular type of entertainment lay in descrying the courtiers beneath their disguises. The basic identity of the courtier and his mask — the dancer and the

dance — had been asserted, as we have seen, even by the early
Tudor disguisings. This was a constant and central idea for
the masque.

What was not constant was the structural unity Crane's
entertainment had offered. It is perhaps unfair to judge from
the youthful king's account, but we may wonder how integral
the masquing was to the debate: what, for example, are the
"friers" and "almaines" doing? Variety, not formal coherence, was the virtue of the late Tudor entertainments. The
dialogue seems to have been regularly separated from the
dancing; we find plays on moral and political themes followed
by masquing and revels with no intrinsic connection between them, serving simply as discrete parts of an evening's
diversion. By the time of Edward VI, Heywood and Nicholas
Udall were providing court drama of a relatively sophisticated type. Except for an occasional pageant, the allegory and
symbolism that filled the early disguisings seem largely to
have been left to the articulate playwrights. The "maskes,"
on the other hand, began to emphasize spectacle for its own
sake and often turned into grotesquerie. Only the titles of
these survive, but they provide adequate characterizations
for our purposes. In 1551, "the masks . . . were of apes and
bagpipes, of cats, of Greek worthies, and of 'medyoxes'
('double visaged, th' one syde lyke a man, th'other lyke
death')." [34] In this year Edward had revived the office of Lord
of Misrule, which had lapsed under his father, and conferred
it on George Ferrers. Possibly it was his influence that re-
sulted in the exoticism of the entertainments: we find
masques of women as Moors (Queen Anne's bright idea for
a "masque of blackness" was by 1605 a very old one), of
Amazons, of covetous men with long noses and torchbearers
with baboon faces, of tumblers dancing on their hands, and
finally, eight days before the young king's death in 1553,
what Ferrers described as "a dronken maske."

These would, of course, have been performed not by courtiers, but by professional entertainers, and we must look on them as providing essentially a different kind of diversion from the courtly disguising, though one easily introduced into it for contrast — an "antic masque" — and as such occasionally used in this period. Grotesquerie and disorder are characteristics of "misrule," and relevant enough to the season of masques and revels. But even in the early disguisings, the antic masque was controlled by a larger structure, superseded — physically, if not always logically — by the court dances. This ordering of misrule was to become the central action of the masque in Ben Jonson's hands. For him the antic dance was an "antimasque" and represented everything that threatened the ideal world of his poem. And there are similar elements, we shall see, in certain Elizabethan masques. Sidney's *The Lady of May* employs a kind of literary antimasque, and we may certainly think of *Proteus* as a work about the controlling of the prototype of disorder. Nevertheless, as far as we can tell, Ferrers' masques were offered with no context, and hence no dramatic and moral implications.

This period must be regarded as a turning point in the history of the masque. Dialogue, which had now become a masque in itself, is the precinct of the poet and has to rely for its effect on drama and verse. So the form gradually takes on the aspect of literature, and this accounts for the enormous variety of Elizabethan masques compared with their Tudor predecessors. It is a variety that approaches chaos if we attempt to find in it a general form, but this is because the conventions it draws on are all the literary ones. The trappings of the early Tudor disguisings are nearly always chivalric; this is an easy metaphor for a court that was still feudal in character — the king was, after all, literally attended by knights and ladies. But the more ambitious Elizabethan masque writers clearly recognized in their audience a reading public. So knights recite Petrarchan sonnets to their

ladies, barriers involve allusions to Malory, the golden world
is viewed more and more frequently as a pastoral rather than
a chivalric one, and even the England of King Arthur is, in
the Elizabethan masques, filled with classical references.

Not that the metamorphosis into poetry took place all at
once. Queen Mary's taste ran to pageantry as well as blood,
and the court that had applauded covetous men with long
noses and "medyoxes" was now entertained with stately and
rich masques of mariners in cloth of gold and silver, of Venetians, of Venuses and Cupids, and so forth. But, in addition,
Mary was interested in drama and employed Nicholas Udall
to provide her court with both plays and masques. Again, we
have little beyond a few titles to tell us what he produced.
But the significant point is that the masque was becoming a
literary form, the province of the dramatist and poet.

3. THE MASQUE AS LITERATURE

It seems trivial to speak of Mary's cultivation of court
drama when we consider that her half-sister witnessed the
flowering of the art; that at the age of nineteen Elizabeth
saw *Gorboduc* and, at sixty-seven, *Twelfth Night*. It was an
art that often made use of elements basic to the masque; the
royal spectator had an active role in *The Arraignment of
Paris* and *Every Man Out of His Humour*, to name only two.
But the entertainments she provided were not lavish in scale,
and in fact the most significant of the Elizabethan court productions were commissioned not by her, but by the subjects
she visited on her numerous progresses. She was diverted and
praised with traditional disguisings and symbolic pageants;
but also, since her progresses were necessarily undertaken
only in spring and summer, the entertainment often became

an outdoor affair, which could last as many days as the royal visit. The season will also help to account for the masque writers' sudden interest in that classic literary mode, the pastoral.

Reports of many of these elaborate affairs remain. As in the conventional masque, the unifying factor is the occasion, the central figure the monarch; and for this reason alone they are relevant to our consideration of the developing form. But since I am primarily concerned here with the background of the Jonsonian masque, Elizabeth's entertainments possess an additional interest precisely because of their literary quality. That Jonson was conscious of them is apparent from the fact that one of his earliest works under King James was a brief but exemplary pastoral entertainment prepared to welcome the new queen and Prince Henry to Althorp in 1603. Jonson was writing in a tradition, and it was, by the beginning of the seventeenth century, a specifically literary tradition. More and more during the Elizabethan years, the texts of court masques tended to be preserved — sometimes, like *Proteus*, chiefly as mementos, but often as serious literature worthy of inclusion in the published works of serious writers.

The earliest extant example of the English masque-as-literature is a wedding masque composed in 1572 by George Gascoigne. His introductory note to the version included in his *Posies* in 1575 is worth pausing over, for it testifies to the overwhelming importance of the occasion and serves to remind us that, from the beginning, the masque writer who thought of himself as a poet was forced to satisfy two very different masters:

There were eight Gentlemen . . . which had determined to present a Maske at the daye appointed for the sayd marriages, and so farre they had proceeded therein, that they had alreadye bought furniture of Silkes, &c., and had caused their garmentes to bee cut of the Venetian fashion. Nowe then they began to imagine that (without some speciall demonstration) it would seeme somewhat obscure to have Venetians presented rather than other countrey men. Whereupon they entreated the Aucthour to devise some verses to bee uttered by an Actor wherein might be some discourse convenient to render a good cause of the Venetians presence.[35]

The poetry here is clearly subservient to the disguising, and Gascoigne is willing enough to accept the terms of his patrons' commission. Nevertheless, to a reading audience he presents his masque as one of the "flowers" of his *Posies*, treating it without apology as a work of literature. The masque itself fulfills its avowed purpose in a thorough but pedestrian way. The Venetians are explained as shipwrecked travelers, members of an Italian branch of the Montacute family, which had commissioned the work. So identified, the masquers could with perfect propriety choose partners from among their cousins in the audience.

Gascoigne's Montacute masque is the first of a series of courtly entertainments with a double purpose, and its main interest lies in its priority. Within a short time, however, more ingenious and imaginative writers were finding in the form an arable if not fertile field for literary expression. We have already considered *Proteus* in some detail. Two other examples will concern us, both with somewhat higher aims than Gascoigne's. The most famous of the Elizabethan entertainments, composed by a variety of hands, was presented at Kenilworth in 1575; and the finest, by Sidney, at Wanstead three years later. I shall concentrate my discussion on these two, asking the reader to bear in mind that there were many others and that, in addition, the court continued to see all the traditional kinds of masques, from pageants to elaborately costumed dances, throughout the age.

Elizabeth visited Kenilworth castle in July 1575 and stayed for nineteen days. Leicester was courting his guest and was determined that her entertainments should lack neither quality nor variety. The theatrical sections were prepared by William Hunnis, Master of the Chapel; George Ferrers, the former Lord of Misrule; Henry Goldingham, a musician and masque writer; and Gascoigne, the best living English poet (Sidney and Spenser had not been heard from yet). The entertainment also included less courtly and more local pleasures, such as folk dancing, sports, and ballad singing. The texts of the festivities were printed by Gascoigne in 1576, under the title *The Princelye pleasures at the Courte at Kenelwoorth*. In addition, we possess a detailed eyewitness account written by a courtier named Robert Laneham to a friend in London. Thus, this entertainment is the first of a small group of works that we are able to consider from both the author's and the audience's points of view.

The most interesting of the sections for my purposes is "the deliverie of the Ladie of the Lake," by Hunnis, presented on the tenth day of the visit, July 18. It begins abruptly, creating its initial effect by ignoring theatrical conventions, by insisting that its action has the same reality as everything else at Kenilworth. This sense is conveyed perfectly by Laneham's letter:

about five a clok her Majesty in the Chase hunted the hart. . . . Well, the game waz gotten: and her highnes returning, cam thear upon a swimming Mermayd . . . Triton, Neptunes blaster: whoo, with hiz trumpet . . . az her Majesty waz in sight, gave soound very shrill & sonorous, in sign he had an embassy to pronoouns.[36]

When the queen reached the bridge over the lake, Triton approached, and in fourteeners (of which Gascoigne thoughtfully provides a prose summary) told "the wofull distress wherein the poore Ladie of the Lake did remaine, the cause whereof was this":

Sir *Bruse, Sauns pittie*, in revenge of his cosen *Merlyne* the Prophet (whom for his inordinate lust she had enclosed in a rocke) did continuallie pursue the Ladie of the Lake: and had (long sithens) surprised hir, but that *Neptune* (pitying hir distresse) had envyroned hir with waves. Whereupon she was enforced to live alwaies in that Poole, and was thereby called the Ladie of the Lake. Furthermore affirming that by *Merlynes* prophecie, it seemed she coulde never bee delivered but by the presence of a better maide then hir selfe. Wherefore *Neptune* had sent him right humbly to beseech hir majestye that she would no more but shew her selfe, and it should bee sufficient to make sir *Bruse* withdrawe his forces.   (102) [37]

With another blast on his trumpet, Triton calls on the forces of nature to be still until the queen has banished Sir Bruse:

> You winds returne into your caves,
>   and silent there remaine:
> You waters wilde suppresse your waves,
>   and keepe you calme and plaine.
> You fishes all, and each thing else,
>   that here have any sway:
> I charge you all in Neptunes name,
>   you keepe you at a stay
> Untill such time this puissant Prince,
>   sir Bruse hath put to flight:
> And that the maide released be,
>   by soveraigne maidens might.   (103)

This invocation, though brief, is in one way the most interesting part of the piece, for it has a certain polish about it, which is rare enough in the age of Tusser, Googe, and Churchyard. Though the verse is plain and the meter a traditionally awkward one, the movement is impressive and dignified. The poem is the work of a writer who has considered the possibilities of language and rhythm with care; and along with the Montacute masque, it provides us with our first textual evidence in a century and a half that the art of poetry was relevant to the composition of courtly entertainments.

The action that Triton has called for, the release of the Lady of the Lake, is now accomplished, although Gascoigne neglects to mention it, presumably because it involves no dialogue. Laneham, however, is as interested in what he saw as in what he heard: "At which petition her highnes staying, it appeerd straight hoow syr Bruse became unseen, his bands skaled, and the Lady by and by, with her too Nymphs, floting upon her moovable Ilands . . . approched toward her highnes on the bridge." [38] She offers her gratitude to Elizabeth, in verse which is again competent if not elegant:

> What worthy thankes, might I poore maide expresse?
> Or thinke in heart, that is not justly due:
> To thee (O Queene) which in my great distress,
> Succours hath sent mine enemies to subdue?
> Not mine alone, but foe to Ladyes all,
> That tyrant *Bruce, Sans Pittie*, whom we call. (104)

Finally, to conclude the work, another messenger of Neptune, "*Protheus* appeared, sitting on a Dolphyns backe. And the *Dolphyn* was conveied upon a boate, so that the Owers seemed to bee his Fynnes. With in the which *Dolphyn* a Consort of Musicke was secretely placed, the which sounded, and *Protheus* . . . sang this song of congratulation." Laneham did not have Gascoigne's text before him and, seeing a musician on a dolphin's back, logically assumed it was Arion. This is a reasonable error for a spectator to make, but from the song itself it is obvious that Gascoigne is correct:

> O Noble Queene give eare,
>   to this my floating muse:
> And let the right of readie will,
>   my little skill excuse.
> For heardsmen of the seas,
>   sing not the sweetest notes:
> The winds and waves do roare and crie
>   where Phoebus seldome floates. (105)

Mysteriously, every modern commentator has accepted Laneham's word rather than Gascoigne's. But surely Proteus, not Arion, is the herdsman of the seas with little skill in music.[39]

Or in poetry, we may wish to add; however, the ubiquitous poulter's measure would have been less tedious with a musical setting.

We can now observe how greatly the Elizabethan audience increased in sophistication. Hunnis knew Proteus only as a minion of Neptune who could be commendably straightforward about the quality of his talents. But by 1595 he had characteristically changed his nature. Davison might have known him as the betrayer of Shakespeare's Valentine and the would-be seducer of Spenser's Florimel. In 1575 the demigod provided the queen's music; twenty years later, he had to be banished before the music could even begin. At Kenilworth Proteus was a benign natural force, and Laneham's error may even suggest the relative gratuitousness of his inclusion in the work: why, after all, not Arion or any one else connected with the sea? At Whitehall, however, he was a poetic convention, and any literate spectator knew exactly what to expect of him.

Indeed, Davison's masque assumes a more literate audience than Hunnis': it is more obviously "composed," more elaborately constructed; it relies more heavily on its rhetoric and on the ability of its audience to follow a complex argument. Nevertheless, in its way *The Ladie of the Lake* is thoroughly literary. Hunnis is not a subtle poet, but his verse shows ease and variety relative to the practice of his time. But literature here has nothing to do with drama: though the work has a fairly complicated plot, the action and the rhetoric are kept rigidly separate. The central event, the destruction of Sir Bruse and his forces, was witnessed by Laneham, but does not appear in Gascoigne's text. The entertainment is conceived as a series of addresses to the queen, invocations to the only figure for whom action is possible. Dramatic interrelationships are wholly absent, and the figures of the masque do not even speak to each other. Everything is directed to Elizabeth, and the verse serves as a commentary on what happens, rather than as a vehicle for it.

Clearly Davison's work is an advance over this. It does employ dialogue, and it makes striking theatrical use of its royal spectator by conceiving the necessary acknowledgment of her presence and power as a revelation that precipitates the main action. Still, it is an advance chiefly in ingenuity — we have already noted how little of *Proteus* is drama, how much exposition and commentary. Despite the elaboration of his rhetoric, Davison, like Hunnis, depends ultimately on nonverbal means to make his point. This has been evident at the climax of both works; it is true in the resolution as well. *The Ladie of the Lake* culminates not with a poem, but with a song. Hunnis' text brings together all nature in a hymn of praise to the chief actor, the monarch as hero. But to our eyewitness the words went unnoticed, and it was the music that dispelled all conflict:

heerwith Arion . . . beegan a delectabl ditty of a song wel apted too a melodious noiz, compoounded of six severall instruments al coovert, casting soound from the Dolphin's belly within; Arion, the seaventh, sitting thus singing (az I say) withoout.

Noow syr, the ditty in miter so aptly endighted to the matter, and after by voys so deliciously deliverd: the song by a skilful artist intoo his parts so sweetly sorted: each part in hiz instrument again in hiz kind so excellently tunabl: and this in the eevening of the day, resoounding from the callm waters: whear prezens of her Majesty, & longing too listen, had utterly damped all noyz & dyn; the hole armony conveyd in tyme, tune, & temper, thus incomparably melodious: with what pleazure (Master Martin), with what sharpnes of conceyt, with what lyvely delighte, this moought pears into the heerers harts, I pray ye imagin yoor self az ye may. . . . As for me, surely I was lulld in such liking, & so loth too leave of, that mooch a doo, a good while after, had I, to fynde me whear I waz.[40]

All but the extravagance of this effect is calculated. Structurally, Proteus' song is analogous to the revels of Davison's masque, as well as to the dancing that in 1527 had concluded *Riches and Love*. For music is integral to the form we are considering and posed yet another problem to the writer who thought of it as a literary form. The masque must conclude with the reassertion of that harmony which has been threatened and of which music is the audible representation. When accompanied by dancing, the representation is visual as well, and dancing was shortly to regain its place as the chief attraction of the court masque. But for Hunnis, and, as we shall see, for Sidney, singing did the work of the revels, turning verse to melody, if not dialogue to choreography.

> Her most excellent Majestie walking in Wansteed Garden, as she passed downe into the grove, there came suddenly among the traine, one apparelled like an honest mans wife of the countrey, where crying out for justice, and desiring all the Lords and Gentlemen to speake a good word for her, she was brought to the presence of her Majestie, to whom upon her knees she offred a supplication, and used this speech.   (329) [41]

So begins *The Lady of May* in the 1598 folio, the basis of all our texts. The title is a modern invention appearing in none of the sixteenth- or seventeenth-century editions. Though running heads are used throughout the 1598 volume, there are none for this work, which concludes the book. And though the work starts on the verso of the last page of *Astrophel and Stella*, there is no catchword for it on the recto. Typographically, in fact, it accosts us with the same abruptness that must have characterized the performance itself. The text has the same sort of immediacy as *Proteus* and *The Ladie of the Lake*: it is intended partly, at least, as a description of the actual production and provides us with a unique record of an audacious experiment that went wrong.

Like Hunnis three years earlier, Sidney insists that the action of his drama has the same kind of reality as everything else at Wanstead. We are turned without warning from a country garden to the world of pastoral, turned, as it were, on a pivot; for, as in the masque, the center is constant, the queen cannot change. But there is no artifice, no frame for the drama, no theater. The actors bring their world with them and transform ours; they deny that they are "characters," treating their audience exactly as they treat each other; and we, as spectators, find we cannot tell them apart from ourselves. We need look no further than this to realize the extent to which *The Lady of May* is conceived in terms of the masque.

The distraught suppliant makes her entreaty directly to the monarch standing before her. The catastrophe is a nuptial; the countrywoman's daughter, the May Lady, has two suitors, a shepherd and a woodsman, and she cannot decide between them. The country people have taken sides, and the Lady's choice now has the aspect of a judgment on the relative merits of two ways of life, the contemplative and the active. It is the queen who must settle the controversy, and the woman urges her to continue her walk, for "your owne way guides you to the place where they encomber her. . . . And with that she went away a good pace, leaving the supplication with her Majestie, which very formallie contained this." The ensuing poem, which I quote in full, was presumably written out and handed to the queen. It seems likely that it was also read aloud, though there is no indication of this in the text. The poem is worth examining, since it exemplifies a rhetorical technique employed throughout the work.

SUPPLICATION

Most gracious Soveraigne,

To one whose state is raised over all,
Whose face doth oft the bravest sort enchaunt,
Whose mind is such, as wisest minds appall,
Who in one selfe these diverse gifts can plant;
     How dare I wretch seeke there my woes to rest,
     Where eares be burnt, eyes dazled, harts opprest?

Your state is great, your greatnesse is our shield,
Your face hurts oft, but still it doth delight,

Your mind is wise, your wisedome makes you mild,
Such planted gifts enrich even beggers sight:
    So dare I wretch, my bashfull feare subdue,
    And feede mine eares, mine eyes, my hart in you.

(330)

The poem is a traditional poetic invocation with this difference: the muse, the inspiration of the work, is literally
present. The masque begins by both invoking and defining
the monarch who is its center, first adducing a set of conventional attributes for her and then qualifying these with
another set. The queen is beyond the reach of ordinary
people, but her greatness is also their comfort and protection.
Though her countenance may be dangerous to look at,[42] it
is also beautiful. Her mind is matchless in argument, but
also wise and understanding. The point to be stressed here
is that both sets of tropes, the initial descriptions and what
subsequently qualifies them, represent traditional attitudes
toward the sovereign. The qualification does not weaken or
deny the original description, but only shows us another aspect of it; the conventions, therefore, remain intact. The
poem, in fact, examining a number of commonplaces about
royalty, speaks wholly in terms of literary conventions, of
stock tropes. It is an apt introduction to the work in that its
rhetorical method, a kind of dialectic of metaphor, is to be
repeated in each of the several debates around which the
drama is built. But we might also note that the masque itself
is conceived as an examination of literary convention — of
one of the basic assumptions of the traditional pastoral.

And yet the work *is* a pastoral. Let us remark from the outset, then, how characteristic it is of its author. Here, as every-
where in his writings, Sidney is above all a critic, and so we
find this masque returning constantly to basic questions of
its own form. *The Lady of May* is concerned with only a
single aspect of the pastoral mode, the assumption that the
contemplative life is more virtuous than the active life. We

may see the critique extended and deepened in the larger pastoral world of *Arcadia*, that wild country where the retired life of the contemplative man is full of deception and misery, and the innocent lover, that indispensable figure of pastoral, is met with sudden and violent death. *Arcadia* is about what happens if we consider the real implications of pastoral romance, about the abrogation of responsibility in a world where nature is not friendly or chance benign. Similarly Sidney creates, in a Petrarchan sonnet sequence, a beloved who is literally unattainable and a lover for whom the sense of loss and separation approaches the Calvinist sense of original sin. Both *Arcadia* and *Astrophel and Stella* are, obviously, serious in a way in which the queen's entertainment at Wanstead cannot be. Nevertheless, the same intelligence is at work, the same sorts of questions are being asked; and the solutions, when they come, are arrived at only after all the traditional assumptions have been discarded. In *The Lady of May*, the validity of the conventional antithesis of pastoral — contemplation versus action — is to be thought through again from the beginning, debated, and judged.

As the action proceeds, the antithesis appears dramatically before us. Immediately after the supplication, "there was heard in the woods a confused noyse, and forthwith there came out six sheapheards with as many fosters haling and pulling, to whether side they they should draw the Lady of May, who seemed to encline neither to the one nor other side." We may wish to call this entry of the "rude upplandisshe people," in its juxtaposition with the decorum of the opening poem, a dramatic antimasque; and certainly we cannot imagine a more striking representation of the central conflict of the drama than a tug of war with the prize in the middle. We become aware at once, however, of the efficacy of the royal presence: "But the Queene comming to the place where she was seene of them, though they knew not her estate, yet something there was which made them startle aside and gaze at her" (330). Let us beware of calling this flattery: its name is convention. There is, simply, that in her countenance which they would fain call master. The validity of the debate, and indeed the whole drama, here hinges on authority, inherent in the nature of the monarch.

Two of the country people now attempt to explain the problem to the queen: Lalus, "one of the substantiallest shepheards," and Maister Rombus, a pedantic schoolmaster. Shepherds are traditionally the heroes of pastoral, and Lalus has been a successful enough shepherd to grow rich at the work. What enlightenment we may justly expect from him, however, is lost in the pretentious ignorance of his euphuism, and he soon yields his place to Rombus who, he says, "can better disnounce the whole foundation of the matter."

Rombus is a scholar. If the shepherd is a conventional exemplar of the contemplative life, Rombus is the contemplative man in person. Yet, far from expounding the basic issues of the masque, his "learned Oration" only succeeds in adding burlesque Latinisms and bombast to the shepherd's periphrases. He barely reaches his subject, taken as he is with both his rhetoric and his accomplishments, and the true and tedious burden of his address is the local contempt for "the pulchritude of my virtues." If the contemplative man is without honor in his own country, then this pastoral land of Sidney's is a most unfamiliar one. In any traditional pastoral, Lalus and Rombus would in some way be at the center of their world, would express at least some truth, embody some virtue that the work may ultimately assert. Here, on the contrary, we find that they cannot even express what the masque is about.

Both are dismissed by the clear, balanced, characteristically Sidneian interruption of the May Lady: "Away away you tedious foole, your eyes are not worthy to looke to yonder Princelie sight, much lesse your foolish tongue to trouble her wise ears." And in this style she proceeds to describe her two suitors, "the one a forrester named *Therion,* the other *Espilus* a shepheard." Espilus is rich, but Therion is lively; Therion "doth me many pleasures," but has a nasty temper, whereas Espilus, though "of a mild disposition," has done her neither any great service nor any wrong. "Now the question I am to ask you," she concludes, "is, whether the many deserts and many faults of *Therion,* or the verie small deserts and no faults of *Espilus* be to be preferred."

The Lady's prose is superseded by a more formal rhetoric as the two adversaries enter to speak for themselves. "Therion chalenged Espilus to sing with him." The ideological conflict is now presented as verbal and musical as well.

> *Espilus.* Tune up my voice, a higher note I yeeld,
> To high conceipts the song must needes be high,
> More high then stars, more firme then flintie field
> Are all my thoughts, on which I live or die:
> Sweete soule, to whom I vowed am a slave,
> Let not wild woods so great a treasure have.
>
> *Therion.* The highest note comes oft from basest mind,
> As shallow brookes do yeeld the greatest sound,
> Seeke other thoughts thy life or death to find;
> Thy stars be fal'n, plowed is thy flintie ground:
> Sweete soule let not a wretch that serveth sheepe,
> Among his flocke so sweete a treasure keepe.
>
> *Espilus.* Two thousand sheepe I have as white as milke,
> Though not so white as is thy lovely face,
> The pasture rich, the wooll as soft as silke,
> All this I give, let me possesse thy grace,
> But still take heede least thou thy selfe submit
> To one that hath no wealth, and wants his wit.
>
> *Therion.* Two thousand deere in wildest woods I have,
> Them I can take, but you I cannot hold:
> He is not poore who can his freedome save,
> Bound but to you, no wealth but you I would:
> But take this beast, if beasts you feare to misse,
> For of his beasts the greatest beast he is.   (333–334)

The singing match is also a formal debate. Therion, the man of action, has issued the challenge. Espilus begins, "as if he had bene inspired with the Muses," but the rebuttal always offers the stronger position in a debate, and Therion clearly knows what he is about. Rhetorically, this duet is set up in the same way as the earlier supplication: Espilus states his case through a series of metaphors, while Therion shows that any trope is only a partial truth.

The shepherd opens in the Petrarchan manner: his love is higher than stars, firmer than earth; he is a slave to his mistress; she is a treasure. The world he adduces is severely limited, and "my thoughts, on which I live or die" turn out to be a set of perfectly conventional conceits. It is precisely the limitations of these metaphors — of this view of the world — that Therion exposes. High notes do not imply high thoughts, and neither are the stars so immutable nor the earth so solid as Espilus imagines. The forester has a much firmer grasp on the physical facts of this pastoral world: Therion's conceits are related directly to apprehensible phenomena — the noise brooks make, falling stars, plowed fields. Indeed, he even has a deeper understanding of the realities of Espilus' life than the shepherd appears to have. Therion uses Espilus' own characterization of himself as a slave to point out that his bondage is more real than he thinks: he is bound to his wealth, his flock. This is Espilus' "treasure," and his metaphor, says Therion, has thus equated his lady with his sheep.

And in his second turn, the shepherd goes on to make the comparison perfectly explicit: "Two thousand sheepe I have as white as milke, / Though not so white as is thy lovely face." The simile, happily, works out to the detriment of the sheep. But the limitations of Espilus' apprehension are now apparent. He boasts of his possessions and conceives of his mistress as one of them; "thy grace" is something he will add to his treasure. Finally we find that it is no longer the lover but the lady who is a slave, for he warns her against *submitting* to the wrong master, "one that hath no wealth."

To Therion, however, possession is a denial of humanity, and his reply, "Two thousand deere in wildest woods I have," is a statement not of his riches, but of his potentialities as a man. Instead of Espilus' wealth, he offers his own freedom and hers; one may keep beasts, "but you I cannot hold." His description of their marriage implies not her submission, but their mutual union. The apostle of wealth, the shepherd, is ultimately seen as only a beast of the higher orders — certainly, at any rate, less than human.

Throughout this exchange, the forester has continually undercut what is for the shepherd his only mode of thought and expression. It is clear that both rhetorically and metaphorically Therion has the better of it. The argument progresses with such ease that we may tend to credit the forester with an easy victory and overlook its significance in the work as a whole. Surely it is unusual to find Espilus, the contemplative man, preaching the virtues of worldly wealth; we had thought it was only in the forest of Arden that shepherds were concerned with economics. But Sidney, like Shakespeare, is redefining the assumptions behind his work, examining and judging the values they imply. Therion has charged Espilus with using conventions he does not understand, with being unaware of the implications of his own metaphors. And the charge is directed as well at the audience at Wanstead, and at us. Essentially, this is the warning of a first-rate critic against abstracting literary devices from their contexts; and it is to become a warning against the dangers of asserting the traditional advantages of the contemplative life, without understanding the function the assertion served in the individual pastorals from which the tradition grew.

The case is discussed more fully in the next debate, a prose parallel to the singing match: "the speakers were *Dorcas* an olde shepheard, and *Rixus* a young foster, betweene whom the schoole-maister *Rombus* came in as moderator." Dorcas speaks for the contemplative view. He cites the legal pro- fession — "the Templars" — as evidence that "templation" is "the most excellent" and sees in the shepherd the man best fitted to a life of contemplation. So, he continues, courtiers leave the court to sit in the country and write pastoral com- plaints about their mistresses. And here, for the first time, we see that the shepherd need not be a literal one: "So that with long lost labour finding their thoughts bare no other wooll but despaire, of yong Courtiers they grew old shep- heards." Their thoughts, contemplation, are their sheep, but in this work even Dorcas is wary of metaphor. Unlike real sheep, he points out, these are unproductive.[43] Finally, the best Dorcas can say for them is that they are utterly harmless. His case rests on sentiment: "he that can open his mouth against such innocent soules, let him be hated as much as a filthy fox."

This is not, even in itself, a very strong argument. But Rixus' rebuttal goes far beyond answering the shepherd's meager claim. Dorcas' life has, he says,

some goodnesse in it, because it borrowed of the countrey quiet- nesse something like ours, but that is not all, for ours besides that quiet part, doth both strengthen the body, and raise up the mind with this gallant sort of activity. O sweet contentation to see the long life of the hurtlesse trees, to see how in streight growing up, though never so high, they hinder not their fellowes, they only enviously trouble, which are crookedly bent. What life is to be compared to ours where the very growing things are ensamples of goodnesse? we have no hopes, but we may quickly go about them, and going about them, we soone obtaine them.
(336–337)

Again, simply by his position in the debate, the foster has a rhetorical advantage. More than that, though, we are aware that no case at all has been presented for the shepherd and that it is Rixus who, in this speech about the virtues of a life of action, is the one really concerned with the life of the mind. "This gallant sort of activity," he says, asserting its inherent nobility, "doth both strengthen the body and raise up the mind"; and his "ensamples of goodnesse" are drawn, like Therion's in the earlier debate, from the observable facts of the pastoral world. One would, I suppose, be hard put to find a *less* active example of the active life than "the hurtlesse trees," but the point is that the man of action is receptive to all experience; he is living as a part of nature, and everything in nature offers him an exemplary lesson. Consequently he, and only he, possesses the contemplative virtues as well. Indeed, we find that for Sidney there can be no dichotomy between contemplation and action: the one necessarily leads to the other. So what we may call "original sin" in *Arcadia* is the renunciation of an active political life for a pastoral dream — which ultimately (and with what pain we learn it!) cannot be realized. We may compare with this the Elizabethan version of a classic invitation to give up the world, couched in the language of Espilus and rejected by the Renaissance prototype of wisdom: "Come, worthy Greek, Ulysses come. / Possess these shores with me."

There can by this time be no question about where the choice between Espilus and Therion must lie. The time for judgment has come, and the May Lady submits her fate to the queen, reminding her and us explicitly "that in judging me, you judge more then me in it." The answer, then, should be a statement about the nature of a whole convention, an apprehension of the kinds of values pastoral may validly assert. Since the case is so clear, we may find it amusing enough that Elizabeth should have picked wrongly, but astonishing that no one since then should have noticed the error. "It pleased her Majesty to judge that *Espilus* did the better deserve her: but what words, what reasons she used for it, this paper, which carrieth so base names, is not worthy to containe" (337).

The omission of the reasoning is perhaps fortunate. Elizabeth, versed in the convention, picked Espilus because shepherds are the heroes of pastoral. But this is a most unconventional pastoral, and how wrong the queen's choice was is apparent from the song of triumph that follows:

> *Silvanus* long in love, and long in vaine,
> At length obtaine the point of his desire,
> When being askt, now that he did obtaine
> His wished weale, what more he could require:
>   Nothing sayd he, for most I joy in this,
>   That Goddesse mine, my blessed being sees.
>
> When wanton *Pan* deceiv'd with Lions skin,
> Came to the bed, where wound for kisse he got,
> To wo and shame the wretch did enter in,
> Till this he tooke for comfort of his lot,
>   Poore *Pan* (he sayd) although thou beaten be,
>   It is no shame, since *Hercules* was he.
>
> Thus joyfully in chosen tunes rejoyce,
> That such a one is witnesse of my hart,
> Whose cleerest eyes I blisse, and sweetest voyce,
> That see my good, and judgeth my desert:
>   Thus wofully I in wo this salve do find,
>   My foule mishap came yet from fairest mind.
>
>   (338)

Espilus, we learn, sang "this song, tending to the greatnesse of his owne joy, and yet to the comfort of the other side, since they were overthrowne by a most worthy adversarie." But the song recounts how Silvanus, the archetype fo(re)ster, *won* his love and how Pan, the archetype shepherd, *lost* his, defeated moreover by Hercules, the archetype man of action. Only the final couplet properly belongs to Espilus, who is clearly the loser.

We may muse a little on the mechanics of this fiasco. The judgment was obviously left entirely in the queen's hands, and it is certainly possible that she was asked to deliver it on the spot. If she saw a text of the work beforehand and prepared her reply, it must have seemed somewhat impolitic for Sidney to tell the learned Eliza that she had missed the point. But why was the final song not revised? — or did the queen withhold her decision even from the author until the performance? If so, did Espilus know Therion's victory song? Or — one final speculation — is the text we have, which was presumably owned by the Countess of Pembroke, simply an original script of the masque, with the queen's decision indicated but not the alterations made for the actual performance?

At last, with a brief valediction, the masquers depart. No curtain closes, there is no theater to leave; nothing has changed, and the queen continues her walk through Wanstead garden. Sidney's problem, like Hunnis', had been to make a queen who was not a masquer the center of his masque. His solution, again like Hunnis', was to conceive his work as a series of addresses to the monarch. But Sidney goes a step beyond his predecessor, for Elizabeth's reply serves as both resolution and critique of the work. So finally rhetoric, not the traditional dance and spectacle, becomes the vehicle for the action of the drama. This looks forward to what Jonson tried to do with the form, to the assertion that, if the masque was a spectacle, it was also a poem. Milton's *Comus* is even more obviously literary, and, like *The Lady of May*, it is highly rhetorical, centers on a debate, and assumes — perhaps equally rashly — that its audience is capable of making the right choice between the contestants. Sidney's essay in the form is a significant step on the way toward these.

Nevertheless, the development was neither easy nor direct. For though Jonson also thought of the masque as didactic, and though his monarch was a spectator, not a dancer, the Jacobean poet's problems were different ones; he had a theater to deal with and illusions to create. Similarly, Davison's *Proteus* has important elements in common with *The*

Lady of May: both are contentions to which the queen provides the solution; both are therefore largely rhetorical. But Davison too has other problems to occupy him, and, insofar as *The Lady of May* is behind *Proteus*, the latter represents a simplification, and perhaps even a retrogression. For example, if we consider the relation between dialogue and dance, and recall Gascoigne's wedding masque of 1572 in which the text is conceived simply as a justification of the dances, we shall see that Davison's greatest debt is not to Sidney. We may remark in *Proteus* the old disunity of rhetoric and action, and think of Kenilworth, not Wanstead. With *Proteus*, moreover, the masque has moved indoors again, and the dances have regained their place as the resolution of disorder.

Had King James's tastes been like those of his predecessor, *Proteus* might have seemed an anomaly. For the move indoors was only a brief one, and Davison's work appears to have generated little enough excitement. Only three masques are recorded as having been performed for Elizabeth after 1595. The one of which we possess a description was a mock joust at barriers and seems to have included no dialogue — a type of entertainment that had maintained its popularity unchanged and undiminished for centuries.[44] Indeed, in *Proteus* we may descry the form of the old Tudor disguising in the ascendancy again. And even the first masque commissioned by the new king, Daniel's *Vision of the Twelve Goddesses* (1604), looks back to the traditional pageant (such as Goldingham's at Norwich in 1578) rather than forward one year to Jonson's *Masque of Blacknesse*. But the traditions of the Tudor spectacle and dance and its Elizabethan mutation into verse and song were both available to the Jacobean court poet who wished to use them; and to the spectacular and theatrical imagination, the increasingly elaborate continental entertainments suggested still other possibilities. Sidney had perfected something new, but the need for it rapidly disappeared. It is primarily the attitude of the artist toward his art that allies Jonson with Sidney, the expectations of his audience that allies him with Davison. In the ensuing pages we must consider both alliances as integral parts of the tradition from which the Jonsonian masque was created.

PART TWO

To Make the Spectators
Understanders

For the first time since the death of Ben Jonson, scholars and critics are beginning to show an interest in his masques as literature. We have come a long way from Gifford's indulgent characterization, "ingenious flattery," of a hundred and fifty years ago, and the epithets we find applied to the masques today often embody sizeable claims for them. The Oxford editors, C. H. Herford and Percy and Evelyn Simpson, are on the whole moderate, but a more recent critic, Dolora Cunningham, is unequivocal about the terms in which she is willing to consider these court productions. "The virtue of princes is to masque," she writes, "as the fall of princes is to tragedy." [1] The only critic of an earlier generation to talk about the masques in this way was Jonson himself; and, in an article considering the masques in the light of Renaissance ethical humanist literature, E. W. Talbert concludes, "Jonson's courtly entertainments are to be interpreted in accordance with his own words, if his purpose and his long preoccupation with the *genre* are to be fully understood." [2]

It is certainly reasonable to take the masques at least as seriously as Jonson took them. And if we are to take his remarks literally, he took them very seriously indeed. But, at the same time, we should be aware that Jonson was a great theorizer after the fact, and it is dangerous to accept indiscriminately his own word for what he was doing. It is a critical commonplace that Jonson's theory of humors does not at all describe the comedy he produced. Similarly, a consideration of his theoretical statements about the masque is no substitute for a reading of the works themselves. For, more significantly in this form than in almost any other, the external requirements of both the commission and the production set the poet's limits and provided his material. And more than any other masque writer, Jonson was able to treat those external requirements as poetic ones, to make of the demands of the occasion a vital element of a complex work of art.

Let me emphasize again, then, that in considering the Jonsonian masque as a literary form, on the one hand, and as an occasional entertainment, on the other, we are not dealing with two independent things, but only with two aspects of the same thing. The masques were commissioned to be produced once or twice or, in rare cases, three times, at great expense for a relatively small and select audience; but the poet makes no apology for the fact that his spectacles are determined by the requirements of that audience. It is one quality of a great writer that the exigencies of his form become not the flaws of his work but its strength. The impossibility of bringing horses onto an Elizabethan stage was transformed by Marlowe into "Holla, ye pampered Jades of Asia: / What, can ye draw but twenty miles a day, / And have so proud a chariot at your heeles." [3] And surely there must have been a double irony in "My kingdom for a horse!" to an audience that knew that the Globe was a world without horses. Similarly, much of the effectiveness of the masques in production would have been inherent in the way Jonson managed to deal with the court he was entertaining and the occasion he was celebrating as integral parts of his spectacle — in short, in the extent to which he was able to unify the disparate parts of the masque form.

The unity was achieved by making occasional necessities into crucial elements of structure — as, for example, Sidney and Davison had already done with the presence of Queen

Elizabeth. But more profoundly than this, the unity was achieved by treating the masque as literature. Jonson went far beyond his predecessors, ultimately making of the masque what he and a few other playwrights had also made of the drama: a work whose text was no longer dependent on its production. The development, despite the general tendencies we have observed throughout the previous century, was not inevitable. Contemporary critics who were shocked at the inclusion of mere plays in the *Workes* of 1616 must have felt even less willing to admit the masque to serious consideration, and Jonson's problem was not only to create a viable literary form, but also to educate his audience to appreciate it. At the same time, because of King James's and Queen Anne's literary and theatrical interests, Jonson was writing much more directly to order than his precursors, and the tastes of his patrons are clearly reflected in the works he produced for them. Not since the time of Henry VIII had the masque been so completely involved with court protocol; and to the artistic conventions of the form were added a whole new set of social conventions to which the poet was required to adapt his invention. It is the process of adaptation that I wish to consider next — the relationship between the poet and his employers and the transformation of their commission into his art. For it is under King James that the really significant changes in the masque take place, and in a way the form is as much the creation of the king's sensibility as of Jonson's.

Whatever reasons Queen Anne may have had for preferring Samuel Daniel to Jonson in 1604, Daniel's first Christmas masque *The Vision of the Twelve Goddesses* must have proved unsatisfactory, for his rival received the commission the following year and regularly thereafter until King James's death in 1625. At the outset of his career as a masque writer, Jonson considered the problems he was faced with and described them in a brief prefatory note to his first masque.

Those inherent in the nature of the form seemed to him most pressing:

> The honor, and splendor of these *spectacles* was such in the performance, as could those houres have lasted, this of mine, now, had been a most unprofitable worke. But (when it is the fate, even of the greatest, and most absolute births, to need, and borrow a life of posteritie) little had beene done to the studie of *magnificence* in these, if presently with the rage of the people, who (as part of greatnesse) are priviledged by custome, to deface their *carkasses*,[4] the *spirits* had also perished. In dutie, therefore, to that *Majestie*, who gave them their authoritie, and grace; and, no lesse then the most royall of predecessors, deserves eminent celebration for these solemnities: I adde this later hand, to redeeme them as well from Ignorance, as Envie, two common evils, the one of *censure*, the other of *oblivion*.   (169:1–14) [5]

The ephemeral nature of the masque concerns Jonson first, and the purpose of his text is to preserve some part of the work of art from destruction. The text, however, is a thing distinct from the work of art; and if, as Jonson implies, the two are only as distinct as spirit and body, nevertheless the body is here of primary importance. It is "in the performance," not in the verse, that "the honor and splendor of these spectacles" chiefly inheres. Thus the masque must be preserved, for it is comparable to "the greatest and most absolute births" and embodies the classic virtue of monarchs, magnificence. Even as Jonson asserts that the role of the poet is essentially a secondary one, he gives that role a new kind of depth and significance, which is conveyed by the very tone of the prose. For the first time, the masque writer is conceiving his function as not merely to celebrate the greatness of his royal spectators, but, like the elegist, "to redeem them as well from Ignorance, as Envie." From the beginning for Jonson, the ephemeral masque involves, paradoxically, a vision of permanence.

In contrast, practical matters — the details of the queen's commission, which at least one contemporary critic found outrageous — pose no problem at all:

PLINY, SOLINUS, PTOLOMEY, and of late LEO the *African* remember unto us a river in *Aethiopia,* famous by the name of *Niger;* of which the people were called *Nigritae,* now *Negro's*: and are the blackest nation of the world . . . Hence (Because it was her Majesties will, to have them [the masquers] *Black-mores* first) the invention was derived by me.   (169:15–23)

Jonson took the external requirement imposed by Queen Anne — that her ladies appear in blackface — and treated it as an organic element of his work of art. The queen's request, in a sense, became the conceit of the masque, and the necessity of fulfilling such requests defines one very important aspect of these productions. "It was her Highnesse pleasure," Jonson writes in *The Masque of Beautie,* the sequel to *The Masque of Blacknesse,* "againe to glorifie the Court, and command, that I should thinke on some fit presentment, which should answere the former, still keeping them the same persons, the daughters of NIGER, but their beauties varied, according to promise, and their time of absence excus'd, with foure more added to their number. To which limits," Jonson continues, "I . . . apted my invention" (181:2–9).

But there were other less explicit requirements to which the masque was "apted" as well. From the first, Jonson shows a remarkably complete awareness of the milieu in which his works were to be presented. He employs perfectly conventional methods — apostrophes to the sovereign, addresses to the audience, symbolic disguises, and the concluding revels — to make the court an essential part of his production; yet the masque he creates takes on a new kind of coherence, and the spectators view it and write about it with a new kind of interest. His sensitivity to his audience — and especially, in the later years, to the tastes of the king — is one quality that sets him off from the rival poets, Daniel, Campion, and Beaumont, and will go far to explain his continued popularity in a court headed by James I. Jonson's ingenuity led him to refine all the familiar devices to establish the traditional union between his masque and its spectators. The sort of solution Davison provided in *The Masque of Proteus* to the problem of the monarch who was not a masquer takes on new life from Jonson's hands. In *The Vision of Delight*, when Wonder asks,

> Whence is it that the ayre so sudden cleares,
> And all things in a moment turne so milde?
>
> (469:174–175)

and Phant'sie replies, gesturing for the first time in the masque directly toward the throne,

> Behold a King
> Whose presence maketh this perpetuall *Spring*,
> The glories of which Spring grow in that Bower,
> And are the marks and beauties of his power,
>
> (469:201–204)

he is performing an action that has been prepared for and even implied by the fact that the center of the masque was King James. It was of course about him, but also, in a purely physical sense, he was its chief viewer: only from his chair did the perspective of the stage achieve its proper effect.[6] Like Davison's Esquire over two decades earlier, Phant'sie is saying that to the sovereign the spectacle owes its existence.[7] But Phant'sie's speech takes into account much more of the situation than the Esquire's, and Jonson's central metaphor is drawn from a larger world and a more complex tradition than Davison was aware of. The idea of the king as sun would not have seemed farfetched to a Jacobean, though it might have seemed entirely conventional — *le roi soleil* was a commonplace even to the seventeenth century. But Jonson has managed to make the convention function dramatically; he has devised a metaphor to express the king's central position in the masque and a fiction within which the metaphor is true.

It was this integrity, this functional relationship between

internal and external exigencies, which made the masque as Jonson conceived it more than a mere spectacle. Jonson was, in effect, treating all the problems of the masque as poetic (or internal) problems. Moreover, although the form was a highly specialized one, its demands were not qualitatively different from those Jonson was meeting in the great amount of occasional verse he composed. In other ways, too, the analogy to poetry is enlightening. The production of the masque was, in a certain sense, the form, the outward shape of Jonson's text; it was the medium through which his invention had to be expressed and the way in which his audience had to perceive it. The two parts of the masque, spectacle and verse, were (as the preface to *Blacknesse* implies) distinct but related entities. Jonson conceived of poetry in the same way, separating the outward form of a poem from its content; for he told William Drummond "that he wrott all his first in prose," and "that Verses stood by sense without either Colour's or accent." [8] It was without hyperbole, then, that he could think of the masque as poetry and demand of it the same order and decorum that he found in the highest art.

4. GREAT PRINCES' DONATIVES

If Jonson was satisfying the queen's pleasure in the masques of *Blacknesse* and *Beautie*, he was less successful in the eyes of other members of the court. That invaluable gossip Sir Dudley Carleton complains of Jonson's first production:

There was a great Engine at the lower end of the Room, which had Motion, and in it were the Images of Sea-Horses with other terrible Fishes, which were ridden by Moors: the Indecorum was, that there was all Fish and no water. At the further end was a great Shell in the form of a Skallop, wherein were four Seats; on the lowest sat the Queen with my Lady Bedford; on the rest were placed the [other] Ladies. . . . Their apparell was rich, but too light and curtezan-like for such great ones. Instead of Vizzards, their Faces and Arms up to the Elbows, were painted black, which was Disguise sufficient, for they were hard to be known; but it became them nothing so well as their red and white, and you cannot imagine a more ugly Sight, than a Troop of lean-cheeked Moors.

And again: "Theyr black faces, and hands . . . was a very lothsome sight, and I am sory that strangers should see owr court so strangely disguised." [9] Miss Welsford notes amusingly that "where Jonson saw a vast sea plowing forth and bearing onwards a strange and wonderful pageant of sea-beings, he [Carleton] saw 'a great engine.' " "Ben Jonson," she adds, "was probably more nearly right than Dudley Carleton." [10] Still, the objections may repay closer attention on our part.

Obviously, Carleton was giving no consideration to the masque as poetry. It will be properly argued that his charge of bad taste is one which the queen must answer, and that the "indecorum" of which he complains is to be found only in what Jonson called "the bodily part. Which was of master Ynigo Jones his designe and act" (172:90–91). Yet the criticisms are just and apply to the poet as well. Carleton cannot forget that, however much the masquers may be Moors, they are also the queen and her ladies. Jonson would agree, at least in principle; his ultimate goal in the masque form was to merge the two characters, to create a symbolic figure that would be an adequate representation of the courtier beneath the mask. This aim is wholly achieved only in certain of the late masques — especially in *Neptunes Triumph* and in the wonderful *The Gypsies Metamorphos'd* — but we can see Jonson working toward it almost from the beginning. And though Carleton's allusion to "indecorum" is obviously a joke (which is, moreover, not really directed at the poet), the remark does touch on a problem that deeply concerned Jonson. To him it was precisely upon the "correctness," the plausibility, the relevance — in short, the seriousness — of these extravagant and fantastic shows that their validity depended.

In the early masques, the relation between Jonson's artifice and the requests of his employers is both direct and rather superficial. *Blacknesse* fulfills the requirements of the queen, but does not, in any deeper sense, take into account the fact that she *is* the queen. Looking at another, but strictly analogous exigency, we might note that the learned annotations to *The Masque of Queenes* were prepared at Prince Henry's request; that the prince's own masque, *Oberon*, includes similar notes, as do all the masques before 1612; but that such annotations are not included in those produced after the prince's death in that year.[11] The omission of this self-conscious learning from the later masques is, in part, merely a natural step in the development of the organic form Jonson sought. But it also reflects the kind of commission the poet was now receiving: for all his scholarship, the king's demands were not those of his eldest son. After 1612, the masques changed accordingly.

There is no evidence that Jonson was writing as directly to order for King James as he had been for the queen and prince. But it is not difficult to derive some idea of James's taste in masques. His pedantry is notorious, and it has often been remarked that Jonson, as a scholar fond of displaying his erudition, would naturally appeal to the king. In a general way, there is no dearth of evidence that James liked Jonson's productions. He regularly provided the Twelfth-Night masque and in 1616 was awarded a pension of a hundred marks for "good and acceptable service done and to be done unto us."[12] In 1619, the year Jonson spent in Scotland, William Drummond wrote him, "I have heard from Court, that the late Mask was not so approved of the King, as in former Times, and that your Absence was regreted: Such Applause hath True Worth, even of those who otherwise are not for it." [13] The masque that appears to have pleased James most was *The Gypsies Metamorphos'd*, which he ordered performed three times during 1621. John Chamberlain wrote to Sir Dudley Carleton,

For lacke of better newes here is likewise a ballet or song of Ben Johnsons in the play or shew at the Lord Marquis at Burly, and repeated again at Windsor, for which and other goode service there don, he hath his pension from a 100 marks increased to 200 li *per annum*, besides the reversion of the mastership of the revells. There were other songs and devises of baser alay, but because this had the vogue and generall applause at court, I was willing to send yt.[14]

There was evidently even talk of a knighthood for the poet.[15] But though the king was clearly delighted, his largesse was mere talk and the knighthood never materialized. The revels reversion could not have meant much to Jonson, since there were two other men in line for the office before him (one of whom outlived him). And as for the two hundred pounds per annum, Chamberlain is sadly mistaken, for in 1629 we find Jonson asking King Charles to raise his pension, which is still one hundred marks, to one hundred pounds.[16] The old king's munificence, as far as Jonson was concerned, lay in the regularity of the yearly commissions and in a general attitude of royal favor.

Only one direct comment of King James's on a Jonson masque has been recorded. Orazio Busino, chaplain to the Venetian ambassador, wrote the following description of *Pleasure Reconcild to Vertue* (1618):

Last of all they danced the Spanish dance, one at a time, each with his Lady, and being well nigh tired they began to lag, whereupon the King, who is naturally choleric got impatient and shouted aloud: "Why don't they dance? What did you make me come here for? Devil take you all, dance." Upon this the Marquis of Buckingham, his Majesty's most favored minion immediately sprang forward cutting a score of lofty and very minute capers, with so much grace and agility that he not only appeased the ire of his angry Lord, but moreover rendered himself the admiration and delight of everybody.[17]

Presumably the king did enjoy other aspects of the masque, but without taking his "choleric" words too literally, we may assume that one of his chief pleasures at these spectacles was watching the dancing — only watching because, unlike the queen and his two sons, he never participated in the masquing. The incident, however, provides us with still more information. "The masque on 12th night," reports Nathaniel Brent to Sir Dudley Carleton, "is not commended of any. The poet is growen so dull that his devise is not worth the relating, much less the copying out. Divers thinke he should returne to his ould trade of bricke laying again." Rarely, indeed, do we find the court gossips so much in agreement. Carleton was deluged with critiques of the spectacle: "the conceit good the poetry not so"; "it came far short of the expectation & Mr Inigo Jones hath lost his reputacion in regard some extraordinary devise was looked for (it being the Prince his first mask) and a poorer one was never sene"; "the invention proved dull." [18] Apparently the king's dissatisfaction was widely shared.

Jonson promptly revised the masque, and from his additions we may gather a good deal about the taste he was writing to suit. *For the Honour of Wales*, the additional material, is a burlesque antimasque to be performed by comic Welshmen. G. E. Bentley correctly observes, "evidently it was thought that the production was not sufficiently splendid to mark the masque debut of Prince Charles." [19] Nevertheless, this is not the objection Jonson is attempting to meet. Comic Welshmen would not add much splendor to a spectacle, but their low comedy could make the difference between failure and success. At the masque's next performance, "it was much better liked than twelveth night," writes the indefatigable

Chamberlain, "by reason of the newe Conceites and Ante-
maskes, and pleasant merry speeches . . . by such as counter-
feited Welse men." [20]

The clearest evidence we have of the king's taste in masques
is to be found here and in the fact that *The Gypsies Metamorphos'd* was his favorite. However little Jonson may have
received materially for the 1621 production, the king was
unequivocal in expressing his satisfaction. Modern readers
have been put off by it, partly because of the masque's dif-
fuseness, but probably more because of the coarseness of its
humor. Herford and Simpson, for example, complain of its
"unsavoury realism." [21] It is often noisily vulgar and less
formal (though certainly no less controlled) than Jonson's
other court masques. It differs also from most of the others
in that its poetry is better — but what the king would have
admired is precisely those qualities of rowdiness and burly
good humor that, perhaps, are less easily conveyed by a
printed version. And it is these qualities, too, that Jonson had
added to *Pleasure Reconcild to Vertue.* Moreover, in *The
Gypsies Metamorphos'd* the problem of relating the masque
world to the world it represents, the world of the court masquers, is handled with an ease and éclat that Jonson rarely attains elsewhere. This problem is a central one for the masque
writer, and his success here would have given the production
a particularly private kind of excitement not to be achieved
in any other type of dramatic presentation.

It is more than a coincidence, considering the king's taste,
that the part of the masque Jonson was most concerned with
during the period 1612–1625 was the antic introductory section, the antimasque. Before 1612, it was characterized by
grotesquerie or melodrama. But from the fantastic witches
of *The Masque of Queenes* (1609) and the delicate indeco-
rousness of *Oberon's* satyrs (1611), Jonson turned gradually
for his antimasques to the material of his plays, to "comedy,
personal satire, and topical allusion," which his Oxford edi-

tors call "disintegrating attractions," but which will be found at the center of Jonson's greatest masques. The antimasque world was a world of particularity and mutability — of accidents; the masque world was one of ideal abstractions and eternal verities. From the time Jonson first conceived of the antimasque as a tiny comic drama in *Love Restored* (1612) the world of accidents began to overshadow the world of essence.

Love Restored opens by avowing itself a mere theatrical production. A masquer enters and speaks:

I would, I could make 'hem a shew my selfe. In troth, Ladies, I pittie you all. You are here in expectation of a device to night, and I am afraid you can doe little else but expect it. Though I dare not shew my face, I can speake truth, under a vizard. Good faith, and't please your Majestie, Your Masquers are all at a stand; I cannot thinke your Majestie wil see any shew tonight, at least worth your patience. . . . The rogue play-boy that acts CUPID, is got so hoarse, your majestie cannot heare him, halfe the bredth o' your chayre. See, they ha' thrust him out, at adventure. We humbly beseech your Majestie to beare with us. We had both hope and purpose it should have been better, howsoever we are lost in it. (377:1–21)

The Cupid who has been thrust out on stage is not the "play-boy," as the masquer assumes, but Plutus, the god of wealth, who has taken on this disguise. The masque world and the court world now begin to merge, as the masquer mistakes a god "under a vizard" for a player. We, however, begin to suspect the error at once.

Plutus. What makes this light, fether'd vanitie, here? Away, impertinent folly. Infect not this assembly.
Mas. How boy!
Plut. Thou common corruption of all manners, and places that admit thee.
Mas. Ha' you recovered your voice, to rayle at me?
Plut. No, vizarded impudence. I am neither player, nor masquer; but the god himselfe, whose deitie is here prophan'd by thee. Thou, and thy like, thinke your selves authoris'd in this

place, to all license of surquedry. But you shall finde, custome
hath not so grafted you here, but you may be rent up, and
throwne out as unprofitable evils. I tell thee, I will have no more
masquing; I will not buy a false, and fleeting delight so deare:
The merry madnesse of one hower shall not cost me the re-
pentance of an age.   (377:22–36)

We have been led with remarkable ease from the world of
the court to the world of fable. Beneath the actor's disguise
and the theatrical illusion lies not everyday life, but the realm
of the antimasque. Plutus' revelation at once renders the fic-
tions of the masque as real as the realities of Whitehall. He
is quintessentially an antimasque figure, for what he attacks
is revelry itself. However wrongheaded his invective, it is
vital and rich; its tone is that of Jonson's finest satirical writing, and it makes of this opening scene the most impressive
part of the work. Indeed, Plutus builds a strong case, apparently striking at his adversaries' weakest point, their extravagance. But the god of wealth defeats himself. He is a
miser; it is he alone who makes a virtue of parsimony and
conceives of morality in terms of buying and selling. He is
revealed at last as a hypocrite, and his puritanical railings
are silenced by the god whose place and appearance he has
usurped, Cupid.

The conflict between riches and love is an old theme for
the masque, and Jonson concludes, like William Crane a
century before, that "both be necessarie for princes." Cupid's
defeat of Plutus is a justification of both liberality and masquing; after the deceptions of the antimasque of riches, the
masque of love presents a symbolic vision of the virtues of
the court and its king. But after the energy of the prose,
Cupid offers verse that is mechanical, and a device hardly
worthy of the ingenuity of the preceding antimasque:

> Imposter *Mammon*, come, resigne
> This bow and quiver; they are mine . . .
> Go, honest spirit, chase him hence,
> To his caves; and there let him dispence,

> For *murders, treasons, rapes*, his bribes
> Unto the discontented tribes;
> Where, let his heapes grow daily lesse,
> And he, and they, still want successe.
>
> (383:227–246)

Nor is the inevitable problem of moving back to the court (the adulation of which is, after all, the basic function of the masque) handled with anything like the ease with which the antimasque moved out of it:

> The Majestie, that here doth move,
> Shall triumph, more secur'd by love,
> Then all his [Plutus'] earth; and never crave
> His aides, but force him as a slave.
> To those bright beames I owe my life,
> And I will pay it, in the strife
> Of dutie backe. See, here are ten,
> The spirits of Court, and flower of men,
> Led on by me, with flam'd intents,
> To figure the ten ornaments,
> That do each courtly presence grace. (384:247–257)

The vital rhythms of Plutus' prose are banished by singsong couplets, as the abstract "spirits of Court" supersede its vividly personified adversary. The weakness of the transition and the vagueness of the world to which it moves us reflect a central problem inherent in Jonson's conception of the masque form.

To the satirist and writer of comedies, it is not ideals but human vice and folly that are eternal. Jonson would naturally be more concerned with what threatens Cupid's realm of absolutes than with "the ten ornaments, / That do each courtly presence grace." Unlike Cupid's realm, the antimasque world is a world of particularity: what impresses us so strongly about Plutus is the variety and inventiveness of his villainous rhetoric. There is nothing abstract about him; he is a dramatic character, an individual, who would fit with ease into a Jonsonian comedy.[22] In contrast, the world of essence, ideal and unchanging, offers little to the dramatic imagination. So Jonson, guided by both his own nature and that of the form he was developing, found in the antimasque the most dynamic part of the masque. Conveniently enough, to this inner requirement of the poet's there was a corresponding external consideration: the king preferred his entertainment comical and indecorous.

In a way, then, the antimasque was the operative element, for which the masque often served merely as a perfunctory epilogue. Yet the form as a whole, both historically and practically, had quite a different function. Its purpose was to glorify the court, and this could only be done within the symbolic masque section. However successful Plutus may be as a dramatic character, he must be confounded if the work is to be a masque. Obviously this is the demand that has not been satisfied in *Love Restored*. We feel an awkward shift of tone with the indispensable gesture toward the throne, "The Majestie, that here doth move"; but a real structural flaw comes with the reference to a dramatic relation between the masque figure Cupid and King James, which has never been established. "To those bright beames I owe my life," says Cupid. But, we are constrained to ask, since when?

In the previous year, in *Oberon*, a similar difficulty had been mitigated (though not, as we shall see, solved) by the fact that the title role was being danced by the crown prince, Henry. The facts of the production were aiding Jonson in establishing those relations between the fable and the court so crucial to the masque. Had the main role in *Love Restored* been conceived for Henry too, his presence beneath the symbolic disguise would have given at least a literal validity to Cupid's claims, though it would not have helped on the fictive level. But the burden of the masque's resolution is a heavy one, and Cupid requires language to carry it. He must, that is, be an actor, and this is a role the courtly masquer cannot play. Prince Henry, the chief courtier here as in *Oberon*, can only dance; conversely, when "the ten ornaments" descend, dance, and take partners from the audience, Cupid does not join them. Even to a contemporary spectator, the poet's failure to establish his central masque figure within the world of the court would have been apparent.

The difficulty in *Love Restored* is a structural one, but it leaves the poet open to an accusation graver than clumsiness. Precisely because the form so directly and intimately includes its audience, any flaw in the transition to the world of the court gives the masque the appearance of tasteless flattery — tasteless, because it involves a violation of artistic decorum; flattery, because it praises a monarch who has never been established as a figure worthy of praise within the masque. When Jonson was wholly successful in fulfilling all the requirements of his form, he could produce works like *Neptunes Triumph* and *Pleasure Reconcild to Vertue*, brilliant examples of his art. We owe it to him to realize that his intention *was* to fulfill both requirements and that the masque was flattery only when it was unsuccessful.

Only two masques were commissioned from Jonson by Charles I, both six years after King James's death. They differ greatly in form and style from any composed for the old king; but evidently they failed to please, for Jonson was not called upon again. This decline in favor is a significant fact if we are examining the relation between the masques and the sovereign for whom they were written. There is much to support the traditional view that it was Inigo Jones's influence with Charles that caused the aging poet's dismissal, though this theory has been tempered by Herford and Simpson and G. E. Bentley. The Oxford editors date the fall from grace from before King James's death, remarking:

even during the last year of the reign, Court influences hostile or indifferent to Jonson had subjected him to some real or apparent slights. During the early summer of 1624, while the fortunes of Prince Charles in Spain still hung in suspense, he appears to have been treated with marked coolness. In particular he was not taken into the secret of the preparations for celebrating the prince's return; a neglect which the author of *Neptune's Triumph* had reason to resent, not the less because this masque, where the splendours of that return were so brilliantly, but illusively, anticipated, had never in fact been performed.[23]

There is a great deal of confusion here. First of all, Charles was in Spain in the summer of 1623 (not 1624), and when he returned on October 6 the Spanish marriage was out of the question. *Neptunes Triumph*, prepared for January 6, 1624, could not, of course, have anticipated a return that had taken place three months earlier. Second, even if we read 1623 for the erroneous date, we must still find it unlikely that a poet being treated by the court with "marked coolness" should receive commissions for three court masques in the space of little over a year. For although a courtier named Sir John Maynard wrote the masque for the prince's return, Jonson did prepare the Christmas masque as usual, and thereafter he supplied the court with *The Masque of Owles* (August 19, 1624) and the masque for the following Christmas, *The Fortunate Isles* (January 9, 1625). King James died in March 1625. So it would seem that we cannot attach very much importance to the fact that Jonson "was not taken into the secret of the preparations" for the prince's return. Indeed, pressing still further, we find that the only masque provided for the celebrations, that of Maynard, was neither commissioned by the king nor performed at court: "It was for Buckingham's own entertainment of the ambassadors, 18 November 1623," notes G. E. Bentley, "that Maynard composed his lost masque." [24] This cannot, then, be taken as evidence of Jonson's decline in favor with the king; but it may imply that the duke and his companion the prince preferred other masque writers.

After James's death, the court did not request Jonson's services for six years. Herford and Simpson point out that "the influences and atmosphere of the new court were on the whole unfavourable to him. The young queen . . . was not likely to be captivated by this 'tun of man.' " Again, "To a man of his [Charles's] delicate and effeminate temperament, acutely resentful of breaches of etiquette and decorum, and shrinking from excesses of every kind, the full-blooded ultra-masculine self-sufficiency and self-assertiveness of Jonson would hardly have been attractive even in an equal." [25] This is perhaps a little overstated, but the point is certainly valid. Bentley, however, proposes an alternative view: "*Loves Triumph Through Callipolis* is Jonson's first masque for the court of Charles I; his last had been for King James six years before in January 1624/5. Perhaps this neglect of the laureate is to be attributed in part to Jonson's paralytic stroke in 1628, but in the early part of his reign King Charles did not provide court masques on the scale his father had." [26] But, if Jonson was still in favor, his illness might more logically have been an occasion for the king's generosity, rather than for his neglect. And it is difficult to see what effect the stroke could have had on the poet's ability to write masques, since he was still able to write new plays, as well as poems asking Charles for money. (*The New Inne*, for example, dates from January 1629.) Moreover, while it is doubtless true that King Charles was less extravagant with court masques than King James had been, Charles did not by any means stint himself. There were two court masques in 1626, two in 1627, and two commissioned for 1628, though not performed. [27] None was by Jonson. The "scale" on which Charles provided masques was evidently high enough to warrant the expense of £1012. 13s. 11d. on one in November 1626, and of £1450 on one in 1628. [28]

It seems reasonable to conclude that the Jonsonian masque simply did not please King Charles. We have some index of the new taste Jonson was attempting to satisfy in the two pieces he finally was called on to compose for the Christmas season of 1630–31, *Loves Triumph Through Callipolis* and *Chloridia*. In these, as in the productions of more esteemed court poets of the age — Carew, D'Avenant, Townshend — the prominence is given to the spectacular aspects of the works. The title pages name "Ben. Jonson. Inigo Jones" jointly as "the inventors." Twenty-five years earlier, the poet had dismissed the designer with a description of his work, concluding, "So much for the bodily part. Which was of master YNIGO JONES his designe, and act." [29] Now, in place of the comic antimasque that Jonson had been developing up to 1625, we find long descriptive paragraphs recounting the argument of the piece, giving lists of the characters, and recording their dances. "All which, in varied, intricate turnes, and involv'd mazes, exprest, make the Antimasque: and conclude the exit, in a circle." [30]

This is all there is of the antimasque in *Loves Triumph*, and Inigo Jones, not Jonson, has provided it. The influence of the Italian-trained architect is evident throughout the work. The number and elaborateness of scene changes bear witness to both his ingenuity and his ascendancy over Jonson. For now, as far as the text is concerned, the whole production is set in the masque world. King James's chief pleasure, it will be remembered, had been in the antimasques. And there is a striking absence of that quality which marks a few of the masques as triumphs of Jonson's art, the vitality which, however controlled by concepts of decorum, is pervasive and operative and stamps this classicist as peculiarly English. It takes many forms, ranging from the rowdy good humor of *The Gypsies Metamorphos'd* to the rich and versatile literary satire of *The Fortunate Isles*; but it is always evident in a general way in Jonson's ability to see as ephemeral a spectacle as the masque in concrete and dramatic terms. This vitality, before 1630, took as its own province the antimasque. In a sense, Inigo Jones, in taking the antimasque from Jonson, had taken the rest of the masque from him as well.[31]

5. THE LIMITS OF INVENTION

The central problem Jonson faced in the masques was to establish the court dramatically within the symbolic world of his spectacle. This was necessary if the adulation, which from the first had been the function of these shows, was to be more than gratuitous flattery. And it was a problem because, properly, the court could be "glorified" only within the masque section; Jonson, for his own reasons, was primarily concerned with the antimasque. Any real success would have to involve a delicate balance between the two — a balance of a sort we do not ordinarily associate with this "tun of man." But for Jonson the masque was a poem as well as a spectacle, so that on the printed page the move into the world of the court became an assertion of those moral virtues of order and nobility that the court embodied. If the crucial transition at Whitehall was not justified, neither was the poetic assertion it represented. It is a remarkable testimony to the integrity of Jonson's imagination that any failure to achieve the necessary unity of form tends to be evident from the quality of the verse in the main masque. *Love Restored* has provided a useful instance: the weak and undefined character of Cupid's poetry implies that something is missing from Jonson's conception of the ideal he is asserting. This is a comparatively simple example. But Jonson had already shown himself capable of producing a type of masque that was more fully imagined and more dramatically realized — and one that was directed as much toward the reader as toward the viewer. Indeed, by 1616, when Jonson presented nineteen masques and entertainments to a reading audience in the first volume of his *Workes*, the success of the masque as literature was clearly of considerable importance.

Taking our cue from the poet, then, let us consider two masques as literary texts — the first, a complex early failure that sets off and illuminates the second, an equally complex success. *Oberon* was composed for the investiture of King James's eldest son, Henry, as Prince of Wales. It was performed on January 1, 1611, with the prince dancing the role of Oberon. In it, Jonson attempts a different kind of dramatic unity from that of *Love Restored*, for *Oberon* is set in an arcadian world large and various enough to contain both antimasque and masque figures.

At the opening of the spectacle,

> *The first face of the* Scene *appeared all obscure, & nothing perceiv'd but a darke Rocke, with trees beyond it; and all wildnesse, that could be presented: Till, at one corner of the cliffe, above the* Horizon, *the* Moone *began to shew, and rising, a* Satyre *was seene (by her light) to put forth his head, and call.* (341:1–5)

This stage direction sets the scene for the antimasque world, characteristically obscure and wild. It is a landscape perceived by the light of the moon, whose inconstancy is invoked and embodied by the wanton satyrs. The discord here is moral as well as physical; the antimasque world is a darker one than that of the revels, in which the moon is Cynthia, "Queene and Huntresse, chaste and faire." [32] Sixteen years earlier, a Shakespearean realm of mischief and passion had been discovered by the same light:

> *Oberon*: Ill met by moonlight, proud Titania.
> *Titania*: What, jealous Oberon! Fairies, skip hence.

But Jonson's Oberon has moved into the masque world, leaving the antimasque to the disorderly creatures of the night.

The satyrs assemble, "leaping, and making antique [antic] action, and gestures." They are presided over by "a Silene," who begins to impose some order upon them. "Chaster language," he urges,

These are nights
Solemne, to the shining rites
Of the *Fayrie* Prince, and Knights.

(343:50–53)

This is simply exposition to us, but in performance it would
have had the kind of dramatic significance peculiar to the
masque form. For *Oberon* was itself part of the "shining
rites" by which the prince beneath the mask was declared
successor to the throne. This special quality is necessarily
lost in a printed version of the masque — and would have
been lost, indeed, in any performance given later than the
particular season for which the masque was composed. The
occasional nature of these shows was both their chief strength
and their ultimate weakness.

But the masque as a poem has its own independent virtues. Jonson's text directs the reader's attention to the prince
by means of a richly imagined dramatic scene. Although
Oberon can have no part in the antimasque, his presence per-
vades it. In verse full of variety and detail, the satyrs excitedly
discuss their expectations of their new ruler, and thereby they
anatomize their world:

> *Satyre 4.* Will he give us prettie toyes,
>   To beguile the girles withall?
> *Satyre 3.* And to make 'hem quickly fall?
> *Satyre 4.* Will he build us larger caves?
> *Silenus.* Yes, and give you yvorie staves,
>   When you hunt; and better wine:
> *Satyre 1.* Then the master of the Vine?
> *Satyre 2.* And rich prizes, to be wunne,
>   When we leape, or when we runne?
> *Satyre 1.* I, and gild our cloven feet?
> *Satyre 3.* Strew our heads with poulders sweet?
> *Satyre 1.* Bind our crooked legges in hoopes
>   Made of shells, with silver loopes?
> *Satyre 2.* Tie about our tawnie wrists
>   Bracelets of the *Fairie* twists?

Satyre 4. And, to spight the coy Nymphes scornes,
　　Hang upon our stubbed hornes,
　　Garlands, ribbands, and fine poesies . . . ?

(344:84–114)

For all their rowdiness, the satyrs speak in beautifully controlled and varied couplets. The indecorum of their antimasque world is full of humor and grace — qualities that, in
theory at least, the advent of a higher good need not destroy.
The relationship between the two parts of Jonson's form is
seen here less as a conflict than as a progression: the satyrs'
anticipation prepares us dramatically for the appearance of
Oberon; but also the very purpose of Silenus is to explain to
his creatures the values of order and constancy, the social
and moral virtues the prince represents. The antimasque
thus becomes, both to its characters and to us, an education
for the concluding revels.

Silenus is a new sort of figure in the Jonsonian masque, for
he comprehends both its worlds. Two years earlier, in *The
Masque of Queenes*, an antimasque of witches had been banished by the "sound of loud Musique . . . with which not
only the Hagges themselves, but theyr Hell, into which they
ranne, quite vanished," and evil had been destroyed by the
mere imminence of good. In *Oberon*, the shift from antimasque to masque takes place not through a momentary
confrontation, but through the gradual ordering of chaos, a
creative act. No mere character can bridge the gap between
the witches' hell and the queens' heaven. But Silenus possesses "all gravitie, and profound knowledge, of most secret
mysteries" (line 50, note c), and he is able to join together the
satyrs and the fairy prince. Under his tutelage, the antimasquers renounce old gods and the wild life: "Grandsire,
we shall leave to play / With Lyaeus now; and serve / Only
OB'RON" (344:77–79). One wonders how many tipsy spectators in 1611 discerned Bacchus beneath the pedantic pseu-
donym Lyaeus and realized uncomfortably that Oberon's

palace was, unlike Whitehall, dry. The satyrs take the pledge
without a whimper, yielding to the promise of better things,
and their moral transformation is rewarded by an analogous
change in the landscape:

> *Silenus.* See, the rocke begins to ope,
>   Now you shall enjoy your hope;
>   'Tis about the houre, I know.
> *There the whole* Scene *opened, and within was discover'd the*
> Frontispice *of a bright and glorious* Palace, *whose gates and walls*
> *were transparent.*   (346:134–140)

We are before the palace of Oberon, the world of the
masque. Silenus continues his explanation:

> Looke! Do's not his *Palace* show
> Like another *Skie* of lights?
> Yonder, with him, live the knights,
> Once, the noblest of the earth,
> Quick'ned by a second birth;
> Who for prowesse, and for truth,
> There are crownd with lasting youth:
> And do hold, by *Fates* command,
> Seats of blisse in *Fairie land.*   (346:143–151)

Even the verse of the antimasque takes on an unfamiliar
regularity. But it is not yet time for the masque figures to appear, since Jonson has related both the moral and physical
transformations of this world to the orderly changes of nature. The satyrs' revels are to end only with the end of moon-
light; in order to "make expectation short," and as a farewell
to their presiding deity, they invoke the unchaste moon with
a satiric song and an antic dance:

> Now, my cunning lady; Moone,
> Can you leave the side, so soone,
> Of the boy, you keepe so hid?
> Mid-wife Juno sure will say,
> This is not the proper way
>   Of your palenesse to be rid.

> But, perhaps, it is your grace
> To weare sicknesse i' your face,
>   That there might be wagers laid,
>   Still, by fooles, you are a maid.
>
> Come, your changes overthrow
> What your looke would carry so;
> Moone, confesse then, what you are.
> And be wise, and free to use
> Pleasures, that you now doe loose;
>   Let us *Satyres* have a share.
> Though our forms be rough, & rude,
> Yet our acts may be endew'd
>   With more vertue: Every one
>   Cannot be Endymion.   (350:262–282)

Jonson concludes his antimasque with a brilliant parody of two central masque conventions, the masquer's invitation to his lady and the final dance. The song inverts all the courtly values: beneath the moon's masquing costume lie inconstancy and wantonness; her "grace" is deception; she is "wise and free" in being licentious; and her lecherous lovers' "acts" are "endew'd with . . . vertue." But the invocation goes unanswered, for the cock crows and the satyrs bow in reverence before the long awaited revelation:

> *Silenus.* Stay, the cheerefull *Chanticleere*
>   Tells you, that the time is neere:
>   See, the gates alreadie spread!
>   Every *Satyre* bow his head.
>
> *There the whole palace open'd, and the nation of* Faies *were discover'd, some with instruments, some bearing lights; others singing; and within a farre off in perspective, the knights masquers sitting in their severall sieges: At the further end of all,* Oberon, *in a chariot, which to a lowd triumphant musique began to move forward, drawne by two white beares, and on either side guarded by three* Sylvanes, *with one going in front.*
>   (351:286–298)

Within the palace is the world of the masque, at once

characterized by triumphant music and pageantry. The dramatic figures, the satyrs of the antimasque, have now become the audience for a symbolic spectacle. Its significance is explained by Silenus and an attendant sylvan, who prepare us for the songs and dances that are to conclude the entertainment and that, to the spectator at Whitehall, were the longest and most important part of the presentation. But, to a reader, such theatrical elements of the work exist only through their literary counterparts; harmony, order, courtliness, grace — the values expressed by music and dance — must be established by Jonson's poetry. So while the characterizations, descriptions, everything that gave substance to the ideal world and its prince, served to justify the revels in performance, they essentially replace the revels when the masque becomes a poem.

Silenus, speaking of Oberon to the satyrs, had described him as a principle of natural beauty and perfection:

> *Satyres*, he doth fill with grace,
>   Every season, ev'ry place;
>   Beautie dwels, but in his face . . .
>   He is lovelier, then in May
>   Is the Spring, and there can stay,
>   As little, as he can decay.   (343:62–73)

It is worth remarking on the fact that the first real difficulty we encounter in the verse arises when Jonson attempts to represent his principle of order. The image of the prince, lovelier than spring, is abstract and conventional to the point of meaninglessness; but it is the sudden obscurity and awkwardness of the poetry that are most striking. The Oxford editors' gloss on "stay As little . . . " — "must advance to further beauty" [33] — is obviously correct. Yet it is surprising that the embodiment of universal order should be defined in verse of so much indirection, so little clarity and ease. Significantly, we come upon precisely the same difficulties again when we reach the ideal world of the masque section.

The opening song establishes a milieu for Oberon's progress toward the ideal. The Platonic ascent becomes a principle of physics and a characteristic of the entire universe:

> Melt earth to sea, sea flow to ayre,
>   And ayre flie into fire,
> Whilst we, in tunes, to ARTHURS chayre
>   Beare OBERONS desire;   (351:300–303)

Nature that framed us of four elements doth teach the prince
to have an aspiring mind — to ascend not only the Platonic
ladder but also "Arthurs chayre," the throne of hereditary
British monarchs. Here is the crucial moment in the masque,
for at this point Jonson must move back into the court; the
heir of "the nation of Faies" must also become the new Prince
of Wales. I quote the whole transition:

> Whilst we, in tunes, to ARTHURS chayre
>   Beare OBERONS desire;
>   Then which there nothing can be higher,
> Save JAMES, to whom it flyes:
> But he the wonder is of tongues, of eares, of eyes.
>   (351:302–306)

The clumsiness of the third and fourth lines, the mysterious
"But" of the fifth, reflect the awkwardness of the transition.
Dramatically, the problem is to identify King James with the
father of the fairy prince, the incarnation of King Arthur.
This is more difficult to effect within the masque than the
identification of Prince Henry with Oberon, because James
was not a masquer whereas the prince was in fact both Oberon
and himself.

The sudden presentation of King James as the object of
the prince's aspiration is like the breach of decorum that had
disturbed Jonson in his *Masque of Queenes*, where Queen
Anne had taken her place among such figures as Penthesilea,
Artemisia, Berenice, and Zenobia. The poet had felt com-
pelled to defend himself from a "possible Objection" by an

appeal to the timelessness of Fame and the "all-daring Power of Poetry" (lines 67off). The objection itself, is of course, trifling and hardly worth such an energetic reply. But obviously Jonson was attempting to deal with the same basic problem: how was the sovereign to be praised *within* the masque?

Now the mention of "Arthurs chayre" would have prepared a court audience or a contemporary reader for a reference to King James, certainly more than it does a modern reader. It was part of the Tudor propaganda program to claim descent from King Arthur, and indeed Jonson several times employs a well-known anagram of the period:

> *Evan.* . . . yow meane his Madestees Anagrams of *Charles James Stuart.*
> *Jenkin.* I, that is *Claimes Arthurs Seate,* which is as much as to say, your Madestee s'ud be the first King of gread Prittan, and sit in Cadier Arthur, which is Arthurs Chaire, as by Gots blessing you doe.[34]

So the allusion to the king at this point in the masque was not a surprise.[35] But this transition from Arthur to James is one that has nothing to do with the *action* of the masque, which would require the king to appear in the symbolic character that has been established for him. The dramatic movement has taken us inward and upward toward the source of light and order, but at the crucial point in the masque this movement has been violated. The masque, in order to be relevant to the real world it symbolizes, must recognize that there is a power higher even than Oberon. Indeed, around the concept of this ultimate power, the object of the prince's aspiration, Jonson has created his masque world. What we end up with, however, is King James, who is not at the center of the masque world, but outside it.

To satisfy the requirements of the production at Whitehall, Jonson had to find a means of including the king in the masque without investing him with properties that, as a spectator, he could not sustain. What goes wrong in *Oberon* is that we are suddenly required to see James enthroned in all his physicality among "bright Faies, and Elves," creatures of no substance "formes, so bright and aery." Thus described, the unfortunate monarch may remind us of Bottom. Conversely, Jonson's problem was to establish Oberon within the world of the court, to bring the masque figure back into Whitehall so that he might serve as a representation of Prince Henry. Until this has been accomplished, praise rendered to Oberon is irrelevant to the prince beneath the mask, and praise rendered to King James is irrelevant to the world the masque has created. This is precisely where *Oberon* fails.

To the reader, therefore, the panegyric of the masque section has the sound of hollow flattery:

> His meditations, to his height, are even:
> And all their issue is a kin to heaven.
> He is a god, o're kings; yet stoupes he then
> Neerest a man, when he doth governe men.
>
> (353:342–345)

There is no synthesis of this praise of the temporal monarch with the following adulation of the ultimate power of the arcadian universe:

> 'Tis he, that stayes the time from turning old,
> And keepes the age up in a head of gold.
> That in his own true circle, still doth runne;
> And holds his course, as certayne as the sunne.
> He makes it ever day, and ever spring,
> Where he doth shine, and quickens every thing
> Like a new nature: so, that true to call
> Him, by his title, is to say, Hee's all. (353:350–357)

The hyperbolic illusion and the real facts have not come together in a moment of revelation; on the contrary, lacking the commanding presence of the king's person or the spectacular effects of the stage production, we feel only that somebody looks ridiculous, that something is being overstated.

Nor are the finest moments in the verse dictated by the dramatic movement of the masque. By requiring us to take its extravagance literally, the verse tends only to undercut the delicate balance between the court world and the symbolic fiction that describes it:

> To whose sole power and magick they doe give
> The honor of their being; that they live
> Sustayn'd in forme, fame, and felicitie,
> From rage of fortune, or the feare to die.
>
> (352:331–334)

Of course, an hour or two of dancing might have given the contemporary spectator sufficient evidence of the fairy knights' substantiality to counteract the disintegrating effects of this sort of hyperbole; and in any case, the necessary illusions were being maintained by the art of Inigo Jones. But neither of these, strictly speaking, was relevant to Jonson's problem, and he had yet found no literary substitute for them. In the masque-poem, Oberon's revels came as a distinct anticlimax.

Of the group of masques Jonson prepared under King James, *Neptunes Triumph for the Returne of Albion* seems to me one of the most successful in dealing with the problems outlined above. It was prepared for Twelfth Night 1624 and celebrated the return of Prince Charles and the Duke of Buckingham from their trip to Spain, where they had attempted to arrange a marriage between the prince and the sister of Philip IV. The project had been understandably unpopular with everyone except the old king and Charles's friends, and the unsuccessful outcome of the negotiations had been a cause for great public rejoicing at the prince's homecoming in October 1623. The masque barely touches on the match, which would have been a sore point, but makes much of the "safe" return of the emissaries. It was never performed, owing to a disagreement over precedence between the Spanish and the French ambassadors; but it was rehearsed up to the last moment, with Charles and Buckingham as the principal masquers.

Like *Love Restored, Neptunes Triumph* opens in the banqueting room at Whitehall; it takes place both literally and figuratively in the court of King James. "All, that is discovered of a *Scene,* are two erected Pillars, dedicated to *Neptune.* . . . The *Poet* entring on the *Stage,*" to distribute handbills of the argument of the masque, "is cald to by the *Master-Cooke.*" The antimasque consists of a discussion between these two of the spectacle the poet has contrived for the evening's entertainment.

The cook demands a description of the coming masque: "Sir, this is my roome, and region too, the banquetting-house! And in matter of feast, and solemnitie, nothing is to be presented here, but with my acquaintance, and allowance to it" (682:24–27). He proceeds to compare his function with that of the poet. "A good *Poet,*" he points out, "differs nothing at all from a *Master-Cooke.* Eithers Art is the wisedom of the Mind. . . . I am by my place, to know how to please the palates of the ghests; so, you are to know the palate of the times: study the severall tastes." And, surprisingly enough, it is the cook, not the poet, who begins to sound most like the Jonson who was King James's masque writer. The poet complains with the voice of one who chafes under the necessity of writing to order: "That were a heavy and hard taske, to satisfie *Expectation,* who is so severe an exactresse of duties; ever a tyrannous mistresse: and most times a pressing enemie" (683:54–56). But the cook urges that the problem must be dealt with, and it is relevant, as the ensuing dialogue shows, not only to the court masque writer, but to any creative artist:

> *Cooke.* She is a powerfull great Lady, Sir, at all times, and must be satisfied: So must her sister, Madam *Curiositie,* who hath as daintie a palate as she, and these will expect.
> *Poet.* But, what if they expect more than they understand?

Cooke. That's all one, Mr. *Poet,* you are bound to satis them. For, there is a palate of the Understanding, as well as the Senses. The Taste is taken with good relishes, the Sight with faire objects, the Hearing with delicate sounds, the Smelling with pure sents, the Feeling with soft and plump bodies, but the Understanding with all these: for all which you must begin at the Kitchin. There, the *Art* of *Poetry* was learnd, and found out, or no where: and the same day, with the *Art* of *Cookery.*

(683:58–73)

The cook is insisting that an appeal to the mind properly involves an appeal to all the senses as well, that poetry cannot be intellectualized, that every resource at the poet's command is to be explored in order to reach the spectator's understanding. Above all, to Jonson, the audience must be made to do more than view the spectacle — they must see the significance of the symbolic figures and of the central device on which the masque depends.

As it continues, this scene between the cook and the poet becomes a dramatic presentation of what Jonson had attempted to achieve through his development of the masque form. Structurally, the function of the Jonsonian antimasque was to set up a world of particularity, which was organically related, and at the same time in contrast, to the symbolic world of the masque. In other words, the antimasque set up a problem for which the masque was a solution. In a very real sense, then, for Jonson it was the antimasque that served to give meaning to the masque, to explain it, to make the audience understand. It is not all surprising that the poet of *Neptunes Triumph,* who has so much trouble with audiences who "expect more than they understand," disapproves strongly of antimasques:

Cooke. But where's your *Antimasque* now, all this while?
　　I hearken after them.
Poet. 　　　　　　　Faith, we have none.
Cooke. None?
Poet. None, I assure you, neither doe I thinke them

> A worthy part of presentation,
> Being things so *heterogene,* to all devise,
> Meere *By-workes,* and at best *Out-landish* nothings.
> *Cooke.* O, you are all the heaven awrie, Sir!
> For blood of *Poetry,* running in your veines,
> Make not yourselfe so ignorantly simple.
>
> (688:213–227)

And it is the cook, finally, who provides the antimasque, both the burlesque dances that immediately precede the main masque and indeed this whole discussion forming the first half of the spectacle. We have already seen how seven years later Jonson, writing to the taste of King Charles, was to omit his own antimasque from *Loves Triumph Through Callipolis* for one of Inigo Jones's devising. So the old poet, deprived of his world of particulars, finds it necessary to prefix a note to that masque entitled explicitly, "To make the Spectators Understanders," which serves to explain the theory on which the masque has been contrived.

Logically, then, the antimasque is the place where the poet of *Neptunes Triumph* sets forth the argument of his masque. We are still in the Banqueting House at Whitehall, and what the poet reads for the cook's approval is an allegorical triumph for the return of Prince Charles to England. The Spanish journey ("through *Celtiberia*") is described: the prince becomes Albion; his father, Neptune; Buckingham (Master of the King's Horse) becomes Hippius, Neptune's "powerfull MANAGER of *Horse*"; Sir Francis Cottington (Charles's private secretary), "*Proteus,* Father of disguise" — Clarendon was to remark of Cottington, "his greatest fault was that he could dissemble."[36] Gradually through the poet's device, we begin to see the court as a mythical realm, and the machines of the masque as examples of Neptune's power and symbols of his grace. The antimasque dialogue prepares us for the transformation scene and serves in a very direct way to make us "understanders":

Cooke.   How do you present 'hem?
    In a fine Iland, say you?
Poet.   Yes, a *Delos*:
    Such as when faire *Latona* fell in travaile,
    Great *Neptune* made emergent.
Cooke.   . . . Ha' you nothing,
    But a bare Island?
Poet.   Yes, we have a tree too,
    Which we doe call the Tree of *Harmonie*,
    And is the same with what we read, the *Sunne*
    Brought forth in the *Indian Musicana* first,
    And thus it growes. The goodly bole, being got
    To certaine cubits height, from every side
    The boughes decline, which taking roote afresh,
    Spring up new boles, & those spring new, & newer,
    Till the whole tree become a *Porticus*,
    Or arched Arbour, able to receive
    A numerous troupe, such as our *Albion*,
    And the Companions of his journey are.
    And this they sit in.
Cooke.   Your prime *Masquers*?
Poet.   Yes.
                              (687:177–211)

However elaborate its symbols, the allegory is nevertheless directly concerned with actual and familiar facts; this, indeed, is its point and chief strength. It is a remarkably inclusive representation of the event that would have been the main topic of conversation in the court for the past three months. Even the delay between the prince's landing in October and the Twelfth-Night masque is dealt with:

> *Cooke.* But, why not this, till now?
> *Poet.*   — It was not time,
>   To mixe this Musick with the vulgars chime.
>   Stay, till th'abortive, and extemporall dinne
>   Of balladry, were understood a sinne,
>   *Minerva* cry'd.   (686:159–165)

There is irony here, for the unsuccessful poet who disdains

antimasques "is not to be identified with Jonson," as the Oxford editors point out. "Jonson himself," they continue, "far from jealously secluding the Poet's courtly music from the 'vulgar's chime' . . . was interweaving the Poet's elegant academic strain with the most genially Epicurean of all his Antimasque-roles — the humours of his 'brother poet,' the Cook." [37]

Herford and Simpson's introduction to *Neptunes Triumph* is excellent, but neither they nor any other commentators appear to have noticed that the relationship between the cook's antimasque and the poet's masque is an organic one. The Oxford editors remark, "The plan of treating Antimasque and Main Masque as rival shows presented by two antagonists of corresponding character was perhaps the most effective of all devices for connecting them." The two sections are more than "rival shows," however; they are complementary and fully embody the Jonsonian concepts of antimasque and masque. The device the poet reads turns the event it deals with into an allegory, takes it into the world of symbolic deities so that it becomes more than the occasion of Prince Charles's return. It is finally a kind of mythical truth, embracing, by the end of the masque, the whole state. By contrast, the cook's antimasque — "a dish out of the kitchen . . . a *metaphoricall* dish!" — presents not truth, but rumor and falsehood. Its dancers emerge from a great stewing pot, dressed as meats of various kinds, appealing in the most obvious way not to "a palate of the Understanding" but to the sensual appetite. These figures represent, as the cook carefully points out, a segment of the court; they are the people who "relish nothing but *di stato*," who gossip endlessly about the business of state,

> Know all things the wrong way, talk of the affaires,
> The clouds, the cortines, and the mysteries
> That are afoot, and, from what hands they have 'hem
> (The master of the Elephant, or the Camels)

What correspondences are held; the Posts
That go, & come, and know, almost, their minutes,
All but their businesse: Therein they are fishes.
But ha' their garlick, as the *Proverb* sayes,[38]
They are our *Quest of enquiry*, after newes.

(689:245–255)

The "relish" with which these figures spread false reports of
court affairs is enough to stamp them as gluttons; and their
characterization through two forgotten proverbs as fish and
garlic easily relegates them to the cook's stewing pot. In this
masque, the antimasquers are those who "know all things
the wrong way," and the deformity of their minds is embodied in the person of the real court figure who is identified
as their leader. He has already been allegorized by the poet
in his summary of his masque as "The Sea-Monster *Archy*"
(line 172), the circulator of "tales and stories" that formed
part of "th'abortive, and extemporall dinne" at Albion's return three months earlier. Archy is Archibald Armstrong,
the court dwarf, who had accompanied the prince to Spain; he
leads the antimasquers as the chief promulgator of false tales,
and his dancers embody whatever in the court world threatens the truths of the poet's allegory.

But the threat need not be destroyed. Antimasque and
masque have a genial relationship in this work, and the cook's
invention can be accepted in the spirit of play and assimilated
with ease into the larger world of the poet's creation.
"Brother Poet," the cook urges, "Though the serious part/
Be yours, yet, envie not the *Cooke* his art." And the poet replies, "Not I. *Nam lusus ipse Triumphus amat*" — even a
triumph likes fun, and the main masque serves less as a rival
show than as the high point of the evening's entertainment.

The striking quality of the opening of the main masque is
that it manages to allegorize the audience and setting along
with the event. We are no longer in the Banqueting House at
Whitehall, but in Neptune's court, watching the landing of

Albion and his train. They come on their floating island; and when "the Island hath joynd it selfe with the shore . . . *Proteus, Portunus,* and *Saron,* come forth, and goe up singing to the State, while the Masquers take time to Land" (693: 361–365). The problem in *Oberon* of incorporating King James in the masque has been solved here; not only is the king addressed as Neptune, but the whole court becomes involved in the transformation. So, when the masquers are ready to take their dancing partners from the spectators, "*Proteus, Portunus, Saron,* goe up to the Ladies with this Song":

> *Pro.* Come, noble *Nymphs,* and doe not hide
> The joyes, for which you so provide:
> *Sar.* If not to mingle with the men,
> What doe you here? Go home agen.
> *Por.* Your dressings doe confesse,
> By what we see, so curious parts
> Of *Pallas,* and *Arachnes* arts,
> That you could meane no lesse.
> *Pro.* Why doe you weare the Silkewormes toyles;
> Or glory in the shellfish spoyles?
> Or strive to shew the graines of ore
> That you have gatherd on the shore,
> Whereof to make a stocke
> To graft the greener Emerald on,
> Or any better-water'd stone?
> *Sar.*   Or Ruby of the rocke?
> *Pro.* Why do you smell of Amber-gris,
> Of which was formed *Neptunes* Neice,
> The Queene of Love; unlesse you can,
> Like Sea-borne *Venus,* love a man?
> *Sar.* Try, put your selves unto't.
> *Chor.* Your lookes, your smiles, and thoughts that meete,
> *Ambrosian* hands, and silver feete,
> Doe promise you will do't.   (697:472–503)

This is a poem about artifice and leads, indeed, to that most complex work of art, the choreography of the revels. But as the three singers examine the nymphs' "arts," it becomes clear that all parts of the natural world, organic and inorganic, terrestrial and aquatic, have contributed to the perfection of this beauty. The verse has an urgency that speeds its lyrical movement. At times it even displays an undercurrent of violence — the toiling silkworms are slaves; the despoiled shellfish, a conquered nation. Images are piled up almost greedily, and not a moment's pause is permitted in the catalogue of riches. As one singer ends, another takes up the theme, and sharp-eyed Saron even adds a gem that Proteus has neglected to mention.

Whitehall has become Neptune's court, and what the sea gods urge is that it is not enough for the audience to be passive observers. In effect, the masque has ceased to be a spectacle and has managed to make its audience integral to its action. Nor has the transition from masque world to court been left to the verse to accomplish, as in *Oberon*; here the synthesis is inherent in the very structure of the work. Just as the failure of *Oberon* had been reflected at the crucial moment in the awkwardness of its poetry, so the success of *Neptunes Triumph* may be measured by the extraordinary grace of the song just quoted. When, shortly afterward, the cook re-enters with a second antimasque of sailors, we find that these dances are no longer threats to the world of the masque, but are now a part of it. The transformation scene is complete.

Among Jonson's masques, there seem to me few successes quite so brilliant as *Neptunes Triumph*, though an examination of several others, notably *Mercurie Vindicated* (1616) and the unfortunate *Pleasure Reconcild to Vertue* (1618), would reveal many of the same qualities. But here we might look briefly at one other, in which the problem of establishing the court within the masque world has been solved in a unique way. *The Gypsies Metamorphos'd* (1621) is particularly interesting because, as I have remarked, it is substantially all antimasque. It was commissioned by Buckingham as part of the entertainment for King James's visit to Burley-on-the-Hill, the duke's country seat. The device calls for a band of gypsies to tell the fortunes of members of the assembled court. The parts of the gypsies were taken by courtiers, with Buckingham in the leading role. The great interest provoked by the masque must have been generated partly by the aptness of the fortunes, but mainly by the rowdy good humor that was so much to the king's taste. There is in the masque no real plot, but only the central contrivance of the fortune telling: the antimasque world needs to employ no symbolic fable in order to be relevant to the world of the court. Hence the fortunes are quite specific in their allusions to particular qualities of the individual courtiers. Reference is made, for example, to the king's dislike of tobacco and pork; and the Countess of Buckingham, the mother of two of the masquers, is reminded that "Two of Your sonnes are *Gypsyes* too" (582:513). All the courtiers are addressed directly and in their own persons. James has been established within the masque by letting him, in effect, represent himself.

We shall respect Jonson's achievement all the more if we examine the masques provided by his rivals under King James. Francis Beaumont, for example, in his *Masque of Gray's Inn and the Inner Temple* (1613), prepared for the wedding of King James's daughter with the Elector Palatine, ignores the problem of relating the audience to the masque world. Aside from the reference embodied in the device — "Jupiter and Juno willing to doe honour to the Mariage of the two famous Rivers Thamesis and Rhene, imploy their Messengers severally, Mercurie and Iris for that purpose" [39] — Beaumont treats his production merely as a spectacular private entertainment with none of the special relevance Jonson attempted to give his masques.

Daniel, whom Jonson had replaced in 1605 as court masquemaker, is aggressively self-effacing about the value and function of his productions. "Whosoever strives to shew most wit about these Pun[c]tillos of Dreames and shews," he writes, "are sure sicke of a disease they cannot hide, and would faine have the world to thinke them very deeply learned in all misteries whatsoever. . . . *Ludit istis animus, non proficit.*" [40] "The mind plays here and does not profit." And, in fact, Daniel's masques were primarily opportunities for his designer to exercise his scenic ingenuity. Daniel made no attempt to achieve the dramatic coherence of the Jonsonian masque, and both *The Vision of the Twelve Goddesses* (1604) and *Tethys' Festival* (1610) are little more than pageantry.

Campion's *Lord Hay's Masque* (1607) does deal directly with the court and attains something like the unity of the best Jonsonian masques. But the difference in quality between this work and the masque as Jonson conceived it lies precisely in the fact that Campion evidently considered blatant flattery indispensable to the form. One example will sufficiently illustrate the point:

> The God of Peace hath blest our land . . .
> We throgh his most loving grace
> A King and kingly seed beholde,
> Like a son with lesser stars
> Or carefull shepheard to his fold. [41]

The hollowness of these alternative epithets for the king is revealed when we try to imagine a masque device whereby James *could* be represented by both the sun and a shepherd at the same time. Campion uses the two images because they are the stock-in-trade of the masque writer: the court is either a pastoral world or the universe. But in *Lord Hay's Masque,* they serve no dramatic or symbolic purpose. We have seen that Jonson's success was in part the result of his ability to use conventions in a functional way. After 1588, for example, to compare England with Neptune's realm was hardly uncommon. But in *Neptunes Triumph,* calling the king a monarch of the seas is not simply hyperbole, for the epithet is inherent in the very device of the masque. It is just this integrity that all three of Campion's court productions lack.

Finally, looking ahead, I should note that, with the possible exception of Chapman, the only contemporary masque writer to conceive of the form in Jonsonian terms appears to have been Milton. *Comus* is frequently adduced as the death blow of the masque, yet in many respects it applied Jonson's technique with a success the earlier poet himself rarely attained. That Milton was constantly aware of his work as a real masque — as a symbolic representation of the milieu in and for which it was created, as a production wherein, when the lords and ladies became masquers, the real world became indistinguishable from the world of the masque — is obvious from the frequency and complexity with which references to his audience, the Earl of Bridgewater and his family and court, are woven into the fabric of the piece. To take only the most striking example, the attendant spirit at the end of his long prologue says that he will disguise himself as "a swain"

> That to the service of this house belongs,
> Who with his soft pipe and smooth dittied song
> Well knows to still the wild winds when they roar,
> And hush the waving woods.

The swain intended is Henry Lawes, the musician of *Comus*, who had obtained the commission for the young poet to write the masque. The spirit compares Lawes to Orpheus in verse that takes on new vividness and strength; but the part of the spirit is, in the production at Ludlow Castle, being played by Lawes himself. What Milton presents, then, is the Lawes of the real world becoming for a time the Lawes of the masque world. The question of flattery is not relevant here, for the disguise — as in Henry VIII's revels, over a century earlier — expresses a basic truth. To Milton, as to Jonson, the function of the court masque is the making of viable myths, whereby courtiers take on the character of heroes, kings of gods, events of symbols. That the myths should be, however incompletely, meaningful for us, too, is the special triumph of the Jonsonian masque.

What I have said should, I think, enable us to view Jonson's masques with some sense of what Jonson was trying to achieve and, therefore, with some sense of what constituted a success in this form. We should be wary, then, of generalizations about "the bondage of tasteless flattery which even the doughtiest of Jacobean poets complacently endured." [42] As for the bondage, the important thing is not that it was there, but that Jonson was able to use it creatively — where Campion, for one, was not. Fetters to a great poet become strengths: "Nuns fret not at their convent's narrow room." And Jonson can hardly be called complacent, when the development of his masques shows a continual, and ultimately successful, effort to establish the praise of the court organically within the masque, where it was valid.

I have withheld a consideration of Jonson's critical comments on the masque until now, since I feel that an understanding of what he was trying to achieve is more likely to be gained by examining what he actually did. But it is certainly relevant that Jonson did theorize about the nature of the masque form. Such remarks appear in various dedications, prefatory notes, and footnotes to the printed versions. In the preface to *Hymenaei*, he speaks of the masque as symbolic poetry. The statement is worth quoting in full:

It is a noble and just advantage, that the things subjected to *understanding* have of those which are objected to *sense*, that the one sort are but momentarie, and meerely taking; the other impressing, and lasting: Else the glorie of all these *solemnities* had perish'd like a blaze, and gone out, in the *beholders* eyes. So short-liv'd are the *bodies* of all things, in comparison of their *soules*. And, though *bodies* oft-times have the ill-luck to be sensually preferr'd, they find afterwards, the good fortune (when *soules* live) to be utterly forgotten. This it is hath made the most royall *Princes*, and greatest *persons* (who are commonly the *personators* of these *actions*) not onely studious of riches, and magnificence in the outward celebration, or shew; (which rightly becomes them but) curious after the most high, and heartie *inventions*, to furnish the inward parts: (and those grounded upon *antiquitie*, and solide *learnings*) which, though their *voyce* be taught to sound to present occasions, their *sense*, or doth, or should alwayes lay hold on more remov'd *mysteries*. And, howsoever some may squemishly crie out, that all endevor of *learning*, and *sharpnesse* in these transitorie *devices* especially, where it steps beyond their little, or (let me not wrong 'hem) no braine at all, is superfluous; I am contented, these fastidious *stomachs* should leave my full tables, and enjoy at home, their cleane emptie trenchers, fittest for such ayrie tastes: where perhaps a few *Italian* herbs, pick'd up, and made into a *sallade*, may find sweeter acceptance, than all, the most nourishing, and sound meates of the world.   (209:1–28)

In part, this seems to be an answer to Daniel's preface to *The Vision of the Twelve Goddesses*, in which he insists on the insubstantiality of such spectacles. But Jonson goes further — he asserts that the masque may be a self-sufficient work of art, for which poetry supplies the essential quality. Jonson is the cook of *Neptunes Triumph*, as well as its poet; he claims that his masques are "full tables," "the most nourishing, and sound meates of the world." He treats his spectacles as poems, and it is therefore relevant to note, as the Oxford editors do, that "He lays down the theory of 'these devices' in the terms which Aristotle applies to the drama." [43] It is perhaps even more important to remark that Jonson was almost alone among contemporary writers in making such claims for the masque. Only Chapman (who, Jonson told Drummond, alone "next himself . . . could make a Mask" [44]) replied to critics of his one court production with a Jonsonian remark: "Every vulgarly-esteemed upstart dares break the dreadful dignity of ancient and authentical poesie." [45]

In 1610, Daniel was obviously attacking Jonson's conception of the form when he wrote in the preface to *Tethys'*

Festival: "And for these figures of mine, if they come not drawn in all proportions to the life of antiquity (from whose tyrannie, I see no reason why we may not emancipate our inventions, and be as free as they, to use our owne images) yet I know them such as were proper to the business, and discharged those parts for which they served, with as good correspondencie, as our appointed limitations would permit." [46] Daniel thinks of the requirements of the form as "appointed limitations" and uses them to excuse whatever his critics may find lacking in his text: the masque (he says in effect) is, after all, not a literary form. But those same limitations became first Jonson's tools and then incidental elements in a much larger structure. So Jonson would hold precisely that his rival's figures were *not* "proper to the business." And we must recognize Jonson's claims because in great measure he substantiated them. He explicitly and continuously worked against the attitude Daniel represented, an attitude that another masquemaker worked into *The Maid's Tragedy*:

> *Lysippus.* Strato, thou hast some skill in poetry; what think'st thou of the masque? Will it be well?
> *Strato.* As well as masques can be.
> *Lys.* As masques can be?
> *Stra.* Yes; they must commend their king, and speak in praise of the assembly, bless the bride and bridegroom in the person of some god; they're tied to the rules of flattery.

Strato's opinion, indeed, appears to have been almost universal. Bacon himself, who (Beaumont tells us) was responsible for the extravagant production of *The Masque of Gray's Inn and the Inner Temple*, remarks of masques and triumphs, "These Things are but Toyes, to come amongst such Serious Observations." The statement is made in an essay of 1625. The Lord Chancellor would have seen a good many of Jonson's masques by then, but he does not appear to have agreed that, "though their *voyce* be taught to sound to present occasions, their *sense*, or doth, or should always lay hold on more remov'd *mysteries*."

Just as it is clear that Jonson alone conceived of the masque as literature, so it is equally clear that this was his primary concern for it. This much is evident from the mere fact that he included his masques in the 1616 edition of his works. Nevertheless, there is a curious uncertainty in his theorizing, as if he did not know quite where to begin to establish his new literary form. In the learned footnotes and prefaces we sense that Jonson somehow felt a need to vindicate his attempt to treat the masques as significant didactic poetry. He explodes straw men:

The twelvth, and worthy *Soveraigne* of all I make *Bel-anna*, Royall *Queene* of the *Ocean*; of whose dignity, and person the whole *scope* of the *Invention* doth speake throughout. . . . But, here, I discerne a possible Objection, arising agaynst mee, to which I must turne: As, *How I can bring* Persons, *of so different* Ages, *to appeare, properly, together? Or, Why (which is more unnaturall) . . . I joyne the living, with the dead?* I answere to both these, at once, Nothing is more proper; Nothing more naturall: For these all live; and together, in theyr *Fame*; And so I present them. Besides, if I would fly to the all-daring Power of *Poetry*, Where could I not take Sanctuary? or in whose *Poëme*? For other objections, let the lookes and noses of Judges hover thick; so they bring the braines: or if they do not, I care not. When I suffer'd it to goe abroad, I departed with my right: And now, so secure an Interpreter I am of my chance, that neither praise, nor dispraise shal affect me.   (*Queenes*, lines 655ff)

He justifies at length the simplest dramatic effects:

[If the witches had explained their purpose] eyther before, or other-wise, it had not bene so naturall. For, to have made themselves theyr owne decipherers, and each one to have told, upon theyr entrance, *what they were, and whether they would,* had bene a most piteous hearing, and utterly unworthy any quality of a *Poeme*; wherein a *Writer* should always trust somewhat to the capacity of the *Spectator*.   (*Queenes*, lines 100ff)

He takes refuge in barely relevant pedantry:

That they [the four humors] were personated in men, hath (alreadie) come under some *Grammaticall* exception. But there is more then *Grammar* to release it. For, besides that *Humores* and *Affectus* are both *Masculine in Genere*, not one of the *Specialls*, but in some Language is knowne by a *masculine* word.
(*Hymenaei*, note to line 112)

But ultimately he speaks of the masque in the specifically moral terms he applies elsewhere to the best poetry:

all Repraesentations, especially those of this nature in court, publique Spectacles, eyther have bene, or ought to be the mirrors of mans life, whose ends, for the excellence of their exhibiters (as being the donatives, of great Princes, to their people) ought alwayes to carry a mixture of profit, with them, no lesse then delight.
(*Loves Triumph*, lines 1ff)

This expresses the same humanistic conviction as the preface to *Volpone*. Jonson is quite explicit, and if we take him literally we shall treat the masques very seriously indeed.

I have already mentioned E. W. Talbert's valuable article, which suggests that we view Jonson's masques as Renaissance ethical-didactic poems: "The voice of Jonson's courtly spectacle, I submit, is that of the panegyric *laudando praecipere*; the sense, that of precepts *de regimine principum* enlarged by the ethical-poetical *credo* of a staunch Renaissance humanist." [47] There is a good deal of validity in this, though the application of Jonson's remarks may be carried too far. For often, examining the masques themselves, we find the symbolic and didactic elements of the masque world a mere perfunctory epilogue to the antimasque. We have seen, for example, that *laudando praecipere* will not at all describe *Oberon*, in which the panegyric and the dramatic elements of the masque work in direct opposition. It is necessary to temper all of Jonson's critical statements with a knowledge of the works in which they appear; the one quoted last above is prefixed to the late *Loves Triumph Through Callipolis* (1631), which has no antimasque. For the masque world alone, the description it offers is apt enough. Yet in attempting to characterize the Jonsonian masque, of course, we can hardly ignore the antimasque.

A brief but admirable statement of the masque's place in its social and courtly context has been given by Jonas A. Barish. The form, he observes,

represents a society not so much aspiring after as joyfully contemplating its own well-being, the possession of the blessings it considers itself to have achieved. The compliments to the king . . . are one expression of this self-congratulation on the part of the community. To eulogize the king is to congratulate the society, of which the king is figurehead, for the communal virtues symbolized in him. To the extent that the actuality falls short of the ideal, the masque may be taken as a kind of mimetic magic on a sophisticated level, the attempt to secure social health and tranquillity for the realm by miming it in front of its chief figure. The frequency of prayer as a rhetorical mode in the masques is hence not accidental.[48]

As it is here summarized, the function of the court masque remained essentially unchanged from its earliest beginnings. Its form, by contrast, seems to be almost infinitely mutable. It is, admittedly, an especially difficult one to define, largely because it involved so many disparate elements. Certainly to the contemporary audience, dancing and spectacle were important attractions of the masque; and what often seems to us a gratuitous addition to a lively antimasque would not have appeared so in seventeenth-century Whitehall. But Jonson was writing for two audiences, treating the non-literary requirements of his form as literary ones, external demands as organic ones. Therefore, if sometimes the main masque with its revels seems perfunctory, this is not merely a mechanical failure in transcribing the spectacle for the reader. It is a structural flaw within the masque itself, such as we have found in *Love Restored* and *Oberon*. In the following pages I shall consider the extent to which Jonson's audience was in fact concerned with dancing and theatrical effects. But even allowing these as the primary interests, we must remember that the masques are also explicitly addressed to another audience, one not in the Banqueting House. Dazzled by the spectacle, the contemporary viewer might well have ignored the literary merits of his evening's entertainment. There is nothing here to justify a similar attitude on our part.

We must read and judge the masques as we read the rest of Jonson's poetry and drama. No matter how much we may use a knowledge of the exigencies of production and the demands of Jonson's position in our effort to understand how and why he should have developed the form as he did, we must be aware at all times that these exigencies were poetic problems to him. What he achieved at his best was a synthesis of the world he wrote for and the world he created.

PART THREE

The Transformation Scene

"At night," wrote Sir Dudley Carleton in 1605, "we had the Queen's Maske in the Banquetting-House, or rather her Pagent." [1] There is more than a fine point of terminology here. *The Masque of Blacknesse* appears to us to have all the qualities that had become characteristic of the form by the end of the sixteenth century. It employs the same basic structure as such standard masques as Gascoigne's Montacute entertainment and Davison's *Proteus*: speeches providing dramatic justification for the entry of masquers and for their dances, which were the main constituents of the evening's show. The fact that Carleton did not see Jonson's and Jones's first production as a masque is interesting enough in itself; but in a larger sense it serves to remind us that audiences and readers see very different things. Jonson felt himself faced with the problem of how "to make the spectators understanders." We may appreciate some of the purely practical difficulties of the poet by considering that the text of *Blacknesse* comprises eleven pages (the length is about average), but that a masque often took three hours to perform.

What, then, does Carleton's distinction imply? The primary elements of the sixteenth-century masque were music and dancing: we have noted that, although the Elizabethans began to see the form in literary terms, on the whole the court entertainment was still the product of the musician, choreographer, and costumer, who employed dialogue, if at all, only incidentally. But a "pagent" in 1605 had more specifically theatrical overtones. "The two main early senses," reports the *Oxford English Dictionary,* "were 'scene displayed on a stage,' and 'stage on which a scene is exhibited or acted.' " Katherine of Aragon's cars with their ship and castle and mount of love were "pageantes proper and subtile," and the term came to be applied to any stage machinery or scenic device. Speeches, we may note immediately, are proper to the stage, though not to the dancing floor. And what Carleton experienced in the Banqueting House on Twelfth Night, 1605, was a theatrical epiphany "which was of master YNIGO JONES his designe, and act." [2]

"First, for the *Scene,* was drawne a Landtschap, consisting of small woods, and here and there a void place fill'd with huntings" (169–170:24–26),[3] which served as a front curtain. In the English public theaters this was a device only for discoveries — what else, after all, was there to conceal? — but it had been common both in sixteenth-century pageants, where the actors on their cars were hidden behind a traverse,[4] and in Italian court performances.[5] It was, however, quite new to the production of masques. Equally new were two other devices of Jones's, which were suddenly revealed when the curtain was released from above and fell to the floor: the stage itself and the perspective scene. These were the trappings of theater and would have impressed the observer more immediately than the subsequent dances proper to a masque.

In addition, several elaborate scenic devices might have reminded Carleton of pageant cars and their attendant shows: "[The curtain] falling, an artificial sea was seene to shoote forth, as if it flowed to the land, raysed with waves, which seemed to move, and in some places the billow to breake. . . . The *Masquers* were placed in a great concave shell, like mother of pearle, curiously made to move on those waters, and rise with the billow" (170:26ff). And later, "*the* Moone *was discovered in the upper part of the house, tri-*

umphant in a Silver *throne . . . & crown'd with a* Lumi-
narie, *or* Sphere *of light. . . . The heaven, about her, was
vaulted with blue silke, and set with starres of* Silver *which
had in them their severall lights burning"* (175, 211ff). Finally,
recalling Carleton's animadversions on the masque itself, and
on the roles played by the queen and her ladies, we may
cull from the *OED* two other contemporary uses of "pageant,"
figurative this time: "Something which is a mere empty or
specious show without substance or reality," and "A part
acted to deceive or impose upon anyone."

"At Night we had the Queen's Maske in the Banquetting-
House, or rather her Pagent." So the remark is both a characterization of a perfectly familiar form as something that
looked quite different to the casual spectator and a critique
of its relevance to the function for which it was designed. It
is important to remember that, however much we may trace
the Jonsonian masque back through an earlier tradition of
entertainments, it was considered from its first appearance
to be something new, striking, and not altogether satisfactory. From the beginning, that is, Jonson's text does not quite
fulfill the exigencies of its production. It is this relationship
we must now consider. We have already examined some aspects of the tension between the poet and his commission
and have arrived at some principles by which the Jonsonian
masque may be judged. Let us now proceed to determine
what the normal form of a masque was for Jonson, and to
what extent it could underlie both what Jonson called "the
mirrors of mans life" and what Inigo Jones called "nothing
else but pictures with Light and Motion."

6. THE QUEEN'S MASQUE

Jonson created his literary form out of a number of non-literary elements, so that within the structure and poetry of his masques we can perceive vestiges of the occasion, setting, music, dancing — sometimes even of the choreography of the dances. The court under James and Charles was particularly fond of masque dances, and contemporary descriptions often dwell at great length on the comparative grace of various courtiers. The dances, then, were integral to the form for Jonson, as they had been for Cornysshe and Crane, but not for, say, Sidney and Goldingham.[6] Equally integral was the new theatricality that impressed Carleton in 1605, and it became increasingly important to both Jonson's and Jones's contributions to the masque form. We shall see why presently; here it is sufficient to note that theater was the one mode of expression that the dramatist and the designer had in common. The Jacobean poet, moreover, faced certain formal problems unknown to his pre-Elizabethan counterparts, and these problems may be seen as logical outgrowths of the development I have traced from the early sixteenth century.

To recapitulate briefly, the Tudor masque was conceived in sections that were dramatically discrete, though symbolically, allegorically, or thematically related: for instance, the dialogue-barriers-dance of *Riches and Love*. Under Elizabeth, the sections became completely separated, and the masque tended to be either wholly literary and dramatic or wholly choreographic and theatrical. Davison's *Proteus* is an uneasy attempt to reunite the elements. But for Jonson the dances were requirements imposed by an agile queen and a king who liked to watch her; and the form was further defined by his own poetic sense, strengthened by the example of Elizabethans like Sidney. It was no longer possible merely to string the elements together in sections. Now both the traditional form provided by the dances and the dramatic form of the poetry became part of one unified structure: the Jonsonian masque.

We may conceive our study of the relationship between Jonson's text and its production as an examination of three elements: the masquing, or disguised dances; the verse and drama; and the *mise en scène* — choreography, poetry, theater. Let us begin with the first, since the dances took most of the time of a masque in performance. The court, we may recall, was used to seeing two kinds of dancing. The first, performed by courtiers, could include a transition to the revels; and the second, by professionals, was most often grotesque or acrobatic in nature. The first is properly a form of social dancing, the talent of every lady and gentleman, and its performers are therefore interchangeable with its audience. The second is theatrical and presupposes an absolute barrier between dancers and spectators. The first is, of course, the more sophisticated development; and we have already noted how under Henry VIII the concept of the court entertainment shifted from that of a show to that of a game.

The distinction between these two types of dancers has moral implications that have survived almost to the present day. Ladies and gentlemen like Gwendolen Harleth and Mr. Rochester preferred playing charades to playing cards, but Fanny Price recoiled in horror at the idea that Mansfield Park might house theatricals, however private. A masquer's disguise is a representation of the courtier beneath. He retains his personality and hence his position in the social hierarchy. His audience affirms his equality with them by consenting to join the dance. This is the climax of the Jacobean masque, and dramatically equivalent to the Tudor unmasking, whereby the symbol opens and reveals the reality. But a professional dancer is like an actor; he plays any part; he can assume all personalities because he has none of his own. Like the courtly masquer, he is identical with his mask, but for a different reason: his persona is not a *representation* of the reality beneath, but the reality itself. When an actor unmasks, the revelation is trivial. We see a person who is no person, who may be anybody, who has been performing an *impersonation*. Whereas the courtier's unmasking is the point of the masque, through which its significance is extended out beyond the boundary of the stage into the real world, the actor's unmasking is the destruction of the dramatic illusion, through which we see that what we have been watching is nothing, a mere trick, a lie — a "pageant." The actor, then, can only exist by limiting himself to the confines of his stage; for once he steps off it, removes his mask, and offers his arm to a spectator, we see him as a mere actor — not like us at all — and no lady can possibly dance with him. This, in fact, is Proteus, who, as Lucian perceived, "is no other than a dancer whose mimetic skill enables him to adapt himself to every character." And he may be overcome, as we have seen, by a confrontation with the prototype of constancy, the pivot on which the masque turns, the monarch. For King Henry is never anything but King Henry; Queen Elizabeth's majesty extends to both spectators and actors; Queen Anne cannot discard her royalty. This is the substance of Carleton's perfectly valid attack on *The Masque of Blacknesse*.

I have already noted some external reasons for Jonson's introduction of the antimasque into the form he was developing. The king loved the sort of humor it involved, and Jonson himself credits Queen Anne with the idea of including "some Daunce, or shew, that might precede hers, and have the place of foyle, or false-Masque" in *The Masque of Queenes* (line 14), though he is quick to add that there is a tradition behind him that he has helped to create. On another level, the antimasque served "to make the spectators understanders" of the transformations and revelations that, dramatically, were the climax of the work, providing (as in *Neptunes Triumph*) not only a foil, but a medium and a means for the action. We may now regard the antimasque from a third point of view and say that Jonson's problem was essentially to unify the *disiecta membra* of the Tudor masque. So the single form, which Jonson conceived in poetic and dramatic terms, had to include dances as well, and dances of both the theatrical and social kinds at that.

We have already seen that the most striking innovation in *The Masque of Blacknesse* was its theatricality. Jonson and Jones met on this ground, and, though it ultimately proved to be an area wider than either had suspected at first, they remained united in recognizing it as basic to their joint creation. The theater and its trappings provided the medium for the Jacobean masque and ultimately, with the development of the proscenium, gave its action a literal frame. So professional actors, personae of the theater, entered the masque, and it was the antimasque that they provided. We have seen how Jonson makes explicit use of the fact that his antimasque players are professionals in *Love Restored*. Just as Jones's theater is from the outset integral to the Jonsonian masque, so is the antimasque with its own type of dance, and for precisely the same reasons: just as the significant movement of the masque is to break through the limits of the stage, so the masquers move the action to a plane on which the antimasquers cannot exist.

We can now begin to see how complex the Jonsonian form was, and how intricately it knit together so many disparate elements. *Blacknesse* is a beginning and has in it the germ of the mature masque. Despite its theatricality, however, its dances are limited to the courtly masquers: its actors only speak and sing. Nevertheless, the text is conceived in terms of antimasque and masque, and Jonson is working clearly within the limits of his tradition. In *The Riche Mount* he could observe that the "action" of his entertainment needed to be no more active than an emblem; in *Proteus*, no more dramatic than a riddle. Around these two devices *The Masque of Blacknesse* is built. As an antimasque, Jonson offers his spectators neither the traditional grotesquerie nor its familiar mutation into dialogue and debate. Instead, a paradox inherent in the very conceit of the work poses the problem the masque must solve.

The title itself is paradoxical, for blackness is a quality antithetical to the court, symbolic source of light and beauty, and to the courtly masquers. The ultimate resolution is achieved only in a sequel, *The Masque of Beautie*. If we think of these two works as standing to each other as antimasque to masque, we shall see that, while Jonson did think in terms of the traditions and conventions of the form, he was nevertheless willing from the outset to go very far afield from the practice of his predecessors.

The world of *Blacknesse* is not, like that of *Oberon*, a place large enough to contain both antimasquers and masquers, satyrs and fairies. That setting is almost a dramatic landscape, but blackness is a symbol, and so is its milieu: a court that is an idealized England, allowing no conflict and no misrule, and where no antimasquers may be admitted. The masquers provide their own antimasque. The conflict of the paradoxical title is carried out in the work not through their actions, but through their mere appearance: the embodiments of beauty are characterized by that quality which to the Elizabethans was a synonym for ugliness. And to a spectator, the action of this Twelfth-Night masque is precisely a series of epiphanies or revelations. It is only necessary that the "twelve *Nymphs, Negro's*" be revealed — that we *see* them — for the "antimasque" to have taken place. Between this revelation and the masque dances and revels, which are still the substance of the entertainment, falls the shadow of the text, which is properly not action but an explanation of the ladies' presence and an analysis of their peculiar problem. We may dwell on this at some length, since it illustrates a method of thinking that is essential to the Jonsonian masque.

Oceanus and Niger, mounted, like Proteus at Kenilworth, on seahorses, lead in the masquers. They are Niger's daughters and appear "in a great concave shell, like mother of pearle," and are welcomed — like Davison's masquers ten years earlier — by the music of tritons and sea maids:

> Sound, sound aloud
> The welcome of the *Orient* floud,
> Into the *West*;
> Fayre NIGER, sonne to great OCEANUS
> Now honord, thus,
> With all his beautious race:
> Who, though but blacke in face,
> Yet, are they bright,
> And full of life, and light.
> To prove that beauty best,
> Which not the colour, but the feature
> Assures unto the creature.   (172:97–108)

They are simply, it seems, too much in the sun. Nevertheless, to any Renaissance aesthetician, color was not essential but merely accidental; and accidents may be disregarded precisely because, by a curiously persistent tautology, they *will* happen. The feature, or form, was of the essence: "For of the soul the body form doth take: / For soule is form, and doth the body make," [7] wrote Spenser when he wished to define beauty. The tritons, good Spenserians, treat the nymphs' blackness as trivial. Niger, on the other hand, when questioned by Oceanus about his presence on "these calme, and blessed shores," asserts the positive values of his daughters' complexions. Pleading his case, Niger sounds very much like Davison's sea god: both believe what they say, and their conviction is based solidly on everything they know of their worlds. Similarly, both figures have the same central dramatic significance; for it is their world views that the masques must repudiate by realizing poetically valid alternatives — ideal worlds where, for example, blackness is not admirable or mutability is not a virtue. But Jonson's sea god is not a villain. He is merely the weary representative of the older generation who never can keep up with his daughters' new fads and is willing to try anything for peace in the household.

Niger's defense of blackness has both logic and the force of a consistent though limited view of nature. He urges first that his daughters' color is evidence of the sun's "fervent'st love,"

> and thereby shewes
> That, in their black, the perfectst beauty growes;
> Since the fix't colour of their curled haire,
> (Which is the highest grace of dames most faire)
> No cares, no age can change; or there display
> The fearfull tincture of abhorred *Gray*;
> Since *Death* her selfe (her selfe being pale and blue)
> Can never alter their most faithfull hiew;
> All which are arguments, to prove, how far
> Their beauties conquer, in great beauties warre;
> And more, how neere *Divinitie* they be,
> That stand from passion, or decay so free.
>
> (173–174:143–154)

The argument is neat, and the tone of the verse supplies a conviction of a sort that was lacking in the last sea god to visit Whitehall. Yet something is wrong. We perceive that Niger must be an antimasque character merely because he is not aware of the paradoxical element in his assumption that blackness is beautiful. Simply, there is something he does not know about his world, and it is expressed by the riddle that has sent the nymphs all over the map and whose solution can turn the antimasquers to masquers:

> That they a Land must forthwith seeke,
> Whose termination (of the *Greeke*)
> Sounds TANIA; where bright *Sol*, that heat
> Their blouds, doth never rise, or set,

But in his Journey passeth by,
And leaves that *Clymat* of the sky,
To comfort of a greater *Light*,
Who formes all beauty, with his sight.

(175:188–195)

To say that Niger cannot answer this riddle is as much as to say that he does not know where he is. We may recall again that this was precisely Proteus' difficulty, and it is one that tends to distinguish antimasquers from masquers. For Davison, once the explanations have been accomplished, the antimasque is over and the triumph of the masque world is at hand. Jonson's imagination is more theatrical, but his device is essentially the same. Here a scenic revelation precedes and parallels the verbal one. Aethiopia, the moon goddess, "was discovered in the upper part of the house," and she serves to conclude the exposition:

Niger, be glad: Resume thy native cheare.
Thy *Daughters* labors have their period here,
And so thy errors. (176:232–234)

Britannia is the land. The nymphs have come to the right place, for it is "Rul'd by a SUNNE"

Whose beames shine day, and night, and are of force
To blanch an AETHIOPE, and revive a *Cor's*.
His light scientiall is, and (past mere nature)
Can salve the rude defects of every creature.

(177:254–257)

What had seemed to Niger evidence of the sun's "fervent'st love" is ultimately a rude defect. The fact is presumably self-evident, for the goddess does not find it necessary to convince Niger of his error and makes her point simply by adducing the remarkable light to which the sun cedes his dominion. The masque world, in fact, is a world of self-evident truths, such as that whiteness is better than blackness or good better than evil. It is only the figures of the antimasque to whom

these are not obvious facts; and we — the audience — are on
the side of the masquers, even as we acknowledge in consenting to dance with them that they are our equals.

Aethiopia must of course, in the speech just cited, gesture
toward the throne. But we shall be doing Jonson some in-
justice if we identify the "light scientiall" simply with King
James. A trope may be perfectly unexceptionable so long as
it is a manner of speaking. If we force it into visual or literal
terms — take it, that is, as a manner of thinking or acting —
we are in danger of arriving at some such ludicrous formula
as "Negroes become white in the presence of the king." The
masque, that poetic world, always ran the risk of becoming
merely an actualized metaphor, and this problem is in certain
ways a particularly Jonsonian one. Let us make a brief excur-
sion into the world of the plays and compare the formula I
have offered above with a not-so-different passage from *The
Staple of Newes*. A lady named Pecunia is complaining of her
guardian to her women, Statute and Band, and her maid,
Waxe:

> *Pecunia.* But once he would ha' smother'd me in a chest,
>   And strangl'd me in leather, but that you
>   Came to my rescue then, and gave mee ayre.
> *Statute.* For which he cramb'd us up in a close boxe,
>   All three together, where we saw no Sunne
>   In one six moneths.
> *Waxe.* A cruell man he is!
> *Band.* H'has left my fellow Waxe out, i' the cold,
> *Statute.* Till she was stiffe, as any frost, and crumbl'd
>   Away to dust, and almost lost her forme.
> *Waxe.* Much adoe to recover me.   (IV.iii.41ff)

This extraordinary exchange represents a *reductio ad ab-
surdum* of the Jonsonian dramatic method. But the masque
precedes the play by twenty years, and it is significant that
the identification of the symbolic figure with the character
who physically represents it is never made in the world of
Blacknesse. The monarch in 1605 is carefully left as an ab-

stract concept: in a kingdom such as the masque postulates, the reigning power may be said to possess all the qualities that are here claimed for it. It is only a paradoxical light that can resolve the paradox of the title. On the other hand, if we wish to be literalistic, we may remark that the sun will bleach as well as burn. This light is not King James; it is, at most, that figure which James, as the center of both the fictive and the actual court, represents. If this seems like a mere dodge on the poet's part, we should recall that the failure to merge the "light scientiall" with the spectator-king is one aspect of a structural problem central to the form, and one that we have already seen Jonson failing to solve six years later in the far more adequately realized world of *Oberon*.

But once the king is identified and the riddle answered, once the nymphs know where they are, the antimasque has given way to the masque. So the revels begin. The moon presents her invitation to the dance, and the ladies descend from the stage to the dancing floor:

Here the Tritons *sounded, and they danced on shore, every couple (as they advanced) severally presenting their fans: in one of which were inscribed their mixt* Names, *in the other a mute* Hieroglyphick, *expressing their mixed qualities.*

(177:266–269)

As the dramatic action yields to the dance, so does the text, which at this point pauses to give the names of the masquers and to enumerate their symbols. For while the drama of the masque properly employs the devices of theater as a means of expression, Jonson has yet found no way to unite the text with the choreography, and thus to make the verse underlie the revels as it had the spectacle. Such unity implies a more complex idea of form than we find in *Blacknesse*; but it is a complexity that Jonson rapidly moves toward, and he achieves it most completely in *Pleasure Reconcild to Vertue* (1618) — a masque explicitly about dancing. In *Blacknesse*, however, the gap between verse and dance is bridged by music that we, to whom the masque is a poem, cannot hear. Instead of the formal activity of the choreography, we find a static list of the masquers and a description of the "mute Hieroglyphick" each presented. For a moment (and let us remember that it is the climactic moment of the masque), this work, which has been developing and analyzing a poetical symbol, renounces the methods of poetry and drama and takes on the aspect of an emblem book. Not until the dance is over can the emblems again become figures in a world we recognize. That world is the world of the theater, which the nymphs have left in order to perform their dance. It is, therefore, significant but not surprising that the music concluding the dance — this time we can hear it, since Jonson has provided a text to go with it — comes from the stage and recalls the dancers to it:

> *Their owne single* dance *ended, as they were about to make choice of their men: One, from the sea, was heard to call 'hem with this* charme, *sung by a* tenor *voyce.*
>
> SONG.
> Come away, come away,
> We grow jealous of your stay:
> If you doe not stop your eare,
> We shall have more cause to feare
> *Syrens* of the land, then they
> To doubt the *Syrens* of the sea.   (178:291–300)

To the masque, it is the real world of the audience that contains the sirens and the rocks on which the fiction may founder; and the song urges the nymphs to return to the safety of the stage and the theatrical illusion. The nymphs, however, not only remain on the floor, but initiate the revels proper:

> *Here they danc'd with their men, severall* measures, *and* corranto's. *All which ended, they were againe accited to sea, with a* song *of two* trebles, *whose cadences were iterated by a double* eccho, *from severall parts of the land.*   (178:301–304)

It takes, in fact, not only the combined forces of these two trebles with their double echoes, but another twenty-five-line harangue from Aethiopia to get the nymphs back to their natural habitat. The goddess concludes her appeal with charms and instructions for the coming year,

> So that, this night, the yeare gone round,
> You doe againe salute this ground;
> And, in the beames of yond' bright *Sunne*,
> Your faces dry, and all is done.   (180:347–350)

What she is saying is that there can be no unmasking yet. This may come as a surprise to the nymphs; certainly for us it is well worth considering carefully.

The dancing section, from the descent of the masquers to their return "to the Sea, where they tooke their Shell," constitutes the theatrical climax of the masque. It has been made possible by the solution of Aethiopia's riddle. And it is interesting that so much has been made of recalling the masquers to the stage, to the fictive world, because we are in danger of believing that with this climax an unmasking *is* possible and that the point of the masque has been reached. But a reader will be aware, more perhaps than a spectator, that answering the riddle does not at all solve the problems the masque has presented. We must realize, that is, that the theatrical climax does not coincide with the poetic or literary one. There are two distinct movements in the masque. One is toward the resolution of the conflict embodied in the unsolved riddle, which stands as a verbal acknowledgment of the fact that the nymphs do not know where they are and that they still belong, therefore, to the world of the antimasque. The proper conclusion of this is the descent, the revels, the shift from antimasque to masque, by which we are to understand that Oceanus has come to the right place at last. The other movement is a more complex one and requires a metamorphosis capable of removing the ladies' blackness, the source of the paradox that has constituted the antimasque. For, again, although through the dances the antimasque world has been left behind, resolving the riddle does not turn the nymphs white, and it is a transformation from blackness to beauty that the text demands. The first movement I have described, then, is theatrical; the second, the metamorphosis, is not.

We have seen here, as always in the masque, that the function of the dialogue is to set things up so that the one significant action constituting the "point" of the masque — and, presumably, its climax — can occur. This action in *Blacknesse,* has split into two clearly defined parts. It is a measure of the immaturity of the work that the two parts do not coincide and that, in fact, there is no stage action corresponding to the real point of the masque. At the theatrical climax of *Blacknesse,* nothing really happens; and the significant action, the metamorphosis of blackness to beauty, takes place *between* the masque and its sequel, *The Masque of Beautie* (1608), in which the nymphs are already white when they appear. Indeed, if we recall that not only three years but two other Twelfth-Night masques intervened between the productions of *Blacknesse* and *Beautie,* we shall perceive that the only place these two bear the proper relationship to each other is in the printed text, where they stand side by side and appear at last as antimasque and masque. Only as literature, that is, do these works achieve their full intended meaning.

We could ask for no better illustration of the basic disparity between the text and the production, poetry and theater, in the Jonsonian masque than *The Masque of Blacknesse.* The poet's problem was to turn this disparity to creative use, to make of it a tension integral to the art form, rather than a threat to its coherence.

7. A SPECTACLE OF STRANGENESS

We have seen that in *Love Restored* (1612), and more significantly in *Neptunes Triumph* (1624), Jonson made explicit use of the theatrical medium as an element of dramatic and poetic structure. In *Oberon* (1611), it was the scene designer's art that was quite literally instrumental in moving us from the outskirts of a recognizable world, "all obscure, & nothing perceiv'd but a darke Rocke, with trees beyond it; and all wildnesse, that could be presented," inward to the center of a society, a palace that presented a Palladian façade and represented a moral order. And we have seen why the trappings of the theater, with its barriers between audience and actors, became the logical means of expression for the antimasque. Insofar as the paradoxical *idea* of a masque of blackness took on the substance of a dramatic reality, then, that substance was wholly defined by the art of Inigo Jones, which provided both a milieu and an instrument for the action. Clearly, too, Jones's theater and the equally basic formal dances, though precisely as disparate by nature as antimasque and masque, worked together as elements of a single unified structure. If we read Jonson's masques in chronological sequence, we shall see him increasingly able to use these nonliterary elements without destroying the work as a literary form.

It seems to me especially important to emphasize this, since it is so often assumed that the masque is simply stage drama *manqué*. For example, M. C. Bradbrook treats the masques as little plays. "It was the invention of the antemasque [*sic*]," she writes, "which enabled Jonson to bring into his Christmas shows . . . a Shakespearean contrast of plot and subplot, reduced to the tiniest scale." [8] But this does not at all describe the relationship of masque to antimasque, for there need be no essential conflict between plot and subplot. Faced with the problem that so many of the masques simply do not look like plays, Miss Bradbrook continues, "His earliest entertainments were filled with allegorical forms, in the strictest Italian taste. The *Masque of Blacknesse* is emblematic." [9] But it is only emblematic when it ceases to work as poetry; and the point about allegory is valuable not because of the Italian influence it implies, but precisely because it emphasizes (though Miss Bradbrook does not) that from the outset Jonson was treating the masque as symbolic poetry. If we pass beyond *Blacknesse* by only four years, to *The Masque of Queenes* (1609), we find Jonson building his piece not around a paradoxical abstraction, but around a group of figures capable of entering into dramatic conflict while retaining their symbolic value. The idea of the masque has crystallized in this short time; theater and dance have already in *Queenes* become instrumental in a way foreign to the very conception of *Blacknesse*.

The introductory description of the 1609 masque is to the point, for in it we see Jonson being perfectly explicit about the nature of his materials. I have already cited the preface to *Hymenaei* (1606), in which Jonson insists on the high seriousness of his purpose in setting forth "these actions." By 1609, the seriousness could presumably be taken for granted. Jonson, at any rate, is a good deal less defensive; and, though perhaps still a little touchy about his status, he is willing to assert the claims of the masque-as-poem merely through a reference to Horace. It is now social decorum that has become the poet's main concern.

It encreasing now, to the third time of my being us'd in these servises to her Majesties personall presentatio's, with the Ladyes whome she pleaseth to honor; it was my first, and speciall reguard, to see that the Nobilyty of the Invention should be answerable to the dignity of theyr persons. For which reason, I chose the Argument, to be, *A Celebration of honorable, & true Fame, bred out of Vertue*: observing that rule of the ª best Artist, to suffer no object of delight to passe without his mixture of profit, & example.

    a. *Hor. in Art. Poetic.* [Jonson's note]   (282:1–9)

The reader will recall that in 1605 Sir Dudley Carleton had found that "the Nobilyty of the Invention" was *not* "answerable to the dignity" of the masquers. Jonson is now aware of the problem and able to deal with it; so much, then, for the genesis of the masque's "Argument." The rest of the description is particularly interesting:

And because her Majestie (best knowing, that a principall part of life in these *Spectacles* lay in theyr variety) had commaunded mee to think on some *Daunce*, or shew, that might praecede hers, and have the place of a foyle, or false-*Masque*; I was careful to decline [afraid of varying] not only from others, but mine owne stepps in that kind, since the last yeare I had an *Anti-Masque* of Boyes: and therefore, now, devis'd that twelve Women, in the habits of *Haggs*, or Witches, sustayning the persons of *Ignorance, Suspicion, Credulity,* &c. the opposites to good *Fame*, should fill that part; not as a *Masque*, but a spectacle of strangenesse, producing multiplicity of Gesture, and not unaptly sorting with the current, and whole fall of the Devise.   (282:10–22)

Here is an embodiment of the moral distinction between theater and revels that I have already described. The witches do not perform a masque, into which the spectator can enter, but a theatrical "spectacle of strangenesse" representing everything we acknowledge to be evil and false, opposed to those self-evident truths upon which the masque world is founded. It is a spectacle we can only watch and from which we must be separated by the boundary at the front of the stage that the actor may not cross. The passage goes on to describe the theatrical machine that sets the limits of the antimasque: "First, then, his Majestie being set, and the whole Company in full expectation, that which presented it selfe was an ougly *Hell*; which, flaming beneath, smoakd unto the top of the Roofe" (282:23–26). It becomes apparent that, like the world of *Blacknesse*, this world has some of the elements of an actualized metaphor. But here the trope has, potentially at least, a dramatic life as well:

And, in respect all *Evills* are (*morally*) sayd to come from *Hell*; . . . These Witches, with a kind of hollow and infernall musique, came forth from thence. First one, then two, and three, and more, till theyr number encreased to Eleven; all differently attir'd; some, with ratts on theyr heads; some, on their shoulders; others with oyntment-potts at their girdles; All with spindells, timbrells, rattles, or other *veneficall* instruments, making a confused noyse, with strange gestures.   (282–283: 26–36)

Briefly we step behind both the scene and the text: "The devise of their attire was *mr Jones his.* with the Invention and *Architecture* of the whole *Scene*, and Machine. only, I praescribd them theyr *properties*, of vipers, snakes, bones, herbes, rootes, and other ensignes of theyr *Magick*, out of the authority of antient, & late *Writers*" (282:36–41). The ancient and late writers, whom Jonson enumerates at length in footnotes, attest to the care with which these ephemeral figures have been created. The masque opens with spectacle, music, and finally, to begin the action, "These eleven Witches beginning to daunce." But the appeals of the text from the start are to poetry and truth.

Shortly after this, Jonson undertakes to defend a dramatic device so elementary that we may suspect it of providing an excuse for a polemic about something else. Unmotivated revelations in drama are, he says,

a most piteous hearing, and utterly unworthy any quality of a *Poeme*: wherein a *Writer* should always trust somewhat to the capacity of the *Spectator*, especially at these *Spectacles*; Where Men, beside inquiring eyes, are understood to bring quick eares, and not those sluggish ones of Porters, and Mechanicks, that must be bor'd through, at every act, with Narrations.
                    (287:104–110)

In part, of course, this is just another smack at Daniel. But, once we have come this far in our study of the masques, the terms of the smack are what is important. For here Jonson is equating "poem" and "spectacle," acknowledging that his audience is of a special kind and that its sensibility is a major consideration in the composition of his masques; and, at a time when he would have been faced most strongly with the limitations of the form, he is affirming its potentialities. He is, in a sense, just beginning to feel at home — the masque world has begun to take on consistency for him.

Theater, music, and dance, then, have set the scene; they are the poet's materials. Let us now consider the action of the masque. The eleven witches assemble on stage and summon their leader with three invocations. "At this, the *Dame* enterd to them" and reveals their purpose, which is, "fraught with spight / To overthrow the glory of this night" (287:111–112). These creatures of the antimasque owe their existence to the world they are committed to destroy, and indeed they have no way of defining themselves except by reference to their antitheses. The speech is worth citing in full, since it puts the Jonsonian antimasque into cosmic terms and will serve to remind us that the masque could be for Jonson a way of talking about the same sort of problem that concerned Spenser and Donne:

> Joyne, now our hearts, we faythfull Opposites
> To *Fame*, & *Glory*. Let not these bright Nights
> Of Honor blaze, thus, to offend our eyes.
> Shew our selves truely envious; and let rise
> Our wonted rages. Do what may beseeme
> Such names, and natures. *Vertue*, else, will deeme
> Our powers decreas't, and thinke us banish'd earth,
> No lesse then heaven. All her antique birth,
> As *Justice, Fayth,* she will restore: and, bold
> Upon our sloth, retrive her *Age of Gold*.
> We must not let our native manners, thus,
> Corrupt with ease. Ill lives not, but in us.

> I hate to see these fruicts of a soft peace,
> And curse the piety gives it such increase.
> Let us disturbe it, then; and blast the light;
> Mixe Hell, with Heaven; and make *Nature* fight
> Within her selfe; loose the whole henge of Things;
> And cause the Endes runne back in to theyr Springs.
>
> (288:132–143)

The witches are characterized by envy, which alone of all the vices can have no proper gratification, but feeds on its opposite and is unable to exist without it. Their ultimate threat, however, is a return to chaos: as always to an Elizabethan the villain is disorder, misrule, Mutability. They defy not only the order of the natural world, but rhetorical and stylistic order as well. They will destroy both the poet's conception and his means of conceiving it, both the spectacle of the masque (which is already apparent, blazing "thus, to offend our eyes") and the verse through which the poet creates, organizes, and controls the world of his poem. To this end, the Dame subverts language, describing her hags in terms that properly belong to the figures of the main masque: they are "faythfull Opposites" and "truely envious," but faith and truth are qualities antithetical to them. Her rhetoric is filled with a tone of righteous exhortation, in sharp contrast to the immoral precepts she offers. A willingness to yield to the power of virtue she calls a corruption of "our native manners," and thereby paradoxically invokes the very concept of nature they are all pledged to destroy.

The Dame speaks in couplets, but her rhetoric typically tends either to disregard or to undercut the organization provided by the form. Note the number of run-on lines where syntactically no pause is possible on the rhyme word. For example,

> Let not these bright Nights
> Of Honor blaze

or

                let rise
        Our wonted rages
or

                Do what may beseeme
        Such names
or

                bold
        Upon our sloth
or

                make Nature fight
        Within her selfe.

There is a basic conflict in the verse between syntax and form,
a conflict of a sort that Jonson often uses merely to produce
rhythmic variations in an extended passage of couplets; but it
could also be invested with moral significance (Donne, he
told Drummond, "for not keeping of accent deserved hang-
ing" [10]) and was therefore very much a device of the antimasque world. In addition, we may perceive in the passage a
secondary rhythmic pattern working to break down the structure of the couplet. It is not simply that the witch speaks in
run-on lines which tend to minimize the ordering effect of
the rhymes, but that time after time the operative rhythmic
unit of the verse is not represented by one line of a couplet.
This will become clear if we consider the following re-
arrangement:

        Joyne, now our hearts,
    We faythfull Opposites to Fame, & Glory.
    Let not these bright Nights of Honor blaze,
    Thus, to offend our eyes. Shew our selves truely
    Envious; and let rise our wonted rages.
    Do what may beseeme such names, and natures.
    Vertue, else, will deeme our powers decreas't,
    And thinke us banish'd earth, no lesse then heaven.
    All her antique birth, as Justice, Fayth,
    She will restore: and, bold upon our sloth,
    Retrive her Age of Gold. We must not let
    Our native manners, thus, corrupt with ease.

The fact that one can rearrange these couplets verbatim into blank verse is not particularly startling; it merely shows that Jonson tended to put his caesuras in the same place in every line. What is significant is that, with only two exceptions, the ends of the lines are also syntactical breaks and therefore require a pause in speaking: the passage above represents the Dame's speech as we would *hear* it. But as the harangue continues — "Ill lives not, but in us" — the movement alters: the spoken and printed texts, the submerged and apparent rhythmic patterns, cease to conflict; the lines become end-stopped, the couplets heroic. For at this point the Dame abruptly changes her methods, shifting her rhetoric from insinuation, subversion of language, and exhortation through a kind of infernal jingoism, to a rhetoric of direct statement and unqualified attack. The shift, in short, is from the rhetoric of propaganda to that of open warfare. The Dame now uses the couplet form to emphasize her points, the rhymes to stress the demands of the syntax.

The effects of the verse are subtle and designed more to be perceived by an auditor than a reader. What a reader may perceive is that the organization of the passage parallels the structure of the masque as a whole, moving stylistically from antimasque to masque. The Dame's invective begins by defining the antimasquers, "faythfull Opposites" to the courtly dancers, and then characterizes the idealized world of the main masque, "these bright Nights of Honor." Her attack next moves outward, beyond the limits of the fiction, to a direct allusion that strikes at the spectators in general and at one in particular: the "soft peace" of line 144 refers to the pacifism around which James I built his foreign policy and of which he was so proud. The remark is a kind of inverted obeisance, a parody of praise. At last the hag includes not only stage and court in her diatribe but the general world as well, just as the masque ultimately presents an image of universal order.

So the hags together recite their charms, urging the "Fiendes, and Furies" to

> Darken all this roofe,
> With present fogges. Exhale Earths rott'nest vapors:
> And strike a blindnesse, through these blazing tapers.
>
> (295:241–243)

That is, they are to destroy the festivities and the world of the impending masque. More incantations follow, until the culmination of the antimasque is reached:

> At which, with a strange and sodayne Musique, they fell into a *magicall Daunce,* full of praeposterous change, and gesticulation, but most applying to theyr property: who, at theyr meetings, do all thinges contrary to the custome of Men, dauncing, back to back, hip to hip, theyr hands joyn'd and making theyr *circles* backward, to the left hand, with strange phantastique motions of theyr heads, and bodyes. (301:344–353)

The witches have been characterized by their costume, by their rhetoric and their singing (the songs of the antimasque are spells and incantations), and now by their manner of dancing, which is contrary to nature, "full of praeposterous change," "a spectacle of strangenesse." This performance parallels the revels of the masque. But the two kinds of dancers are here mutually exclusive, and the stage is not large enough to contain them both.

These figures cannot be converted to the service of Good Fame, as the satyrs two years later were to come to serve Oberon. The world of *Queenes* is one of moral absolutes, and the witches' commitment to evil is a total one: "Ill lives not," they say, "but in us"; and the corollary is, if not in us, then nowhere. (Indeed, they have no other terms, no way of conceiving of themselves except as the opposites of the queens who are the masquers.) They must, therefore, totally disappear before the masquing can begin. And here Jonson faces his first major structural problem: how is the principle of evil to be disposed of?

In the antimasque, action had been effected by the power of verse — the hags sing and their Dame appears. But it takes an Inigo Jones to exorcise disorder and metamorphose the scene: the age of gold is also perforce an age of machines. The masques of 1605 and 1608 had no way of representing the change from blackness to beauty. By 1609, Jonson has found a means of expressing the transformation, though as yet he can do little more than describe it:

> In the heate of theyr *Daunce*, on the sodayne, was heard a sound of loud *Musique*, as if many Instruments had given one blast. With which, not only the *Hagges* themselves, but theyr *Hell*, into which they ranne, quite vanishd; and the whole face of the *Scene* alterd; scarse suffring the memory of any such thing: But, in the place of it appear'd a glorious and magnificent Building, figuring the *House of Fame*, in the upper part of which were discoverd the twelve *Masquers* sitting upon a Throne triumphall, erected in forme of a *Pyramide*, and circled with all store of light. From whome, a Person, by this time descended, in the furniture of Perseus; and expressing *heroïcal*, and *masculine Vertue* began to speake.   (301–302:354–366)

The universe of the main masque is a Platonic one. In the kind of world Jonson has set up, the queens are absolutes and the hags their antitheses — everything that, in the sublunary world, denies and threatens the ideal. No progression from antimasque to masque can take place through dramatic means, for drama implies interaction and conflict. But the world of the witches does not conflict with the world of the queens; on the contrary, it negates and contradicts it. So the very essence of drama is here unavailable to Jonson: his antagonists, absolute good and absolute evil, cannot by their very natures confront each other on a stage and resolve their discord. The transition from the world of abstract vice to that of abstract virtue is one which no mere figure in the masque can make. "Doctrine" (Jonson might have recalled from Spenser) is "much more profitable and gratious . . . by ensample, then by rule." [11] But Jonson offers us only the rule:

his masque world is not yet large enough to contain an exemplary figure who acts and learns.

The masque is persuading us to a very old truth about the Platonic universe, but it is a truth that even Plato accepted largely on faith. Socrates *was* able to convince Meno that man naturally desires good and need only perceive it in order to follow it; the argument, however, assumes that good is simply that which man desires to follow. When the argument is stated in more abstract terms, and the hypothetical man omitted, both the proposition and its circularity become less obvious: Evil is powerless in the presence of Good. But Socrates' point was a small link in a long chain, and the "man" was all-important. It is he who does the acting, desires good or is deceived by the appearance of evil, and thus provides whatever drama is implicit in the Platonic example. Jonson objectifies the Socratic abstractions, and the figures of his drama are the two poles between which the now nonexistent agent had moved. Yet, though they have become dramatis personae, Good and Evil cannot confront each other, conflict, interact, because their nature forbids it. No drama, then, is possible, since the one figure capable of moving between the worlds of metamorphosis and mutability, capable, in short, of dramatic action, has been left out of the masque.

This is why nothing happens in *The Masque of Queenes*, why it can only present two discrete, antithetical sections whose point of contact is not drama or verse, but "a sound of loud Musique" and an elaborate scene shift. I have already remarked that Jonson's next masque, *Oberon*, does contain a character who can bridge the gap between antimasque and masque — who can allow the masque to achieve its climax through drama rather than through music and spectacle.

The main masque is a new world, presided over by Heroic Virtue and Fame. Inigo Jones's machine has transformed not only the theater's "ougly Hell," but our own world as well.

The House of Fame has many mansions, and one of them is evidently the palace at Whitehall, for Heroic Virtue is able to address King James directly and in his own person — and thus, incidentally, to undo the antimasque's slight to the royal policy:

> To you, most royall, and most happy King,
> Of whom *Fames* house, in every part, doth ring
> For every vertue; but can give no' increase:
> Not, though her loudest Trumpet blaze your peace.
>
> (304:432–435)

The speeches are, as we might expect, largely in heroic couplets ("for," Jonson told Drummond, "he detesteth all other Rimes" [12]), and they introduce a procession of historical and mythological queens culminating, like Goldingham's pageant at Norwich in 1578, in the real queen herself. There is, of course, no text for these, since, being masquers, they only appear (their mere appearance implies the defeat of the witches), dance, and take partners. "Imagine the *Masquers* descended," the poet urges us,

and agayne mounted, into three triumphant *Chariots*, ready to come forth. The first foure were drawne with *Eagles*. . . . theyr 4 Torchbearers attending on the *chariot* sides, and foure of the *Hagges*, bound before them. Then follow'd the second, drawne by *Griffons*, with theyr Torch-bearers, and foure other *Haggs*. Then the last, which was drawne by *Lions*, and more eminent (Wherin her Majestie was) and had six Torch-bearers more, (peculiar to her) with the like number of Hagges. After which, a full triumphant *Musique*, . . . while they rode in state, about the stage.   (314:710–721)

The revels come as the celebration of a triumph, almost as a ritual, for which no dramatic explanation is necessary. Jonson, having eschewed drama in the structure of the masque, can hardly be expected to be concerned about why the ladies descend. They dance, because that is what they are there for. It is only in the antimasque, that world of conflict and change, that the problem of dramatic motivation seems to Jonson a significant one.

As the hags had been defined by their dancing, so are the queens by theirs:

> they daunc'd theyr third *Daunce*; then which a more *numerous* composition could not be seene: *graphically* dispos'd into *letters*, and honoring the Name of the most sweete, and ingenious *Prince, Charles, Duke of Yorke* Wherin, beside that principall grace of perspicuity, the motions were so even, & apt, and theyr expression so just; as if *Mathematicians* had lost *proportion*, they might there have found it.   (315–316:749–756)

One of the things the witches embodied was ignorance. The masque dances here are a form of wisdom, as they are in *Pleasure Reconcild to Vertue* and in a more famous Renaissance poem about dancing, Davies' "Orchestra."

Here then is one central way in which the Jonsonian masque has moved beyond the conception of the form represented by *Blacknesse* and *Beautie*. The poet has begun to use nonliterary elements, the dances, functionally in the work; and *Queenes* thus displays a new sort of coherence. But choreography is only one of the ways in which the masque speaks to the spectator. The most meaningful antithesis we can find in the work is the simple contrast between the verse of the antimasque and that of the masque. We have already examined an extended expository passage; but since most of the witches' poetry is incantation, let us consider a more representative selection. In it, we shall see Jonson's masque poetry already taking on an expressive suppleness uniquely suited to the form and to be found nowhere else in his works. Here are the opening stanzas:

> Sisters, stay; we want our *Dame*.
> Call upon her, by her name,
> And the charme we use to say,
> That she quickly' anoynt, and come away:

1. CHARME.

Dame, Dame, the watch is set:
Quickly come, we all are met.
From the lakes, and from the fennes,
From the rockes, and from the dennes,
From the woods, and from the caves,
From the Church-yards, from the graves,
From the dungeon, from the tree,
That they die on, here are wee.
Comes she not, yet?
Strike another heate.

2. CHARME.

The Weather is fayre, the wind is good,
Up, *Dame,* o' your Horse of wood:
Or else, tuck up your gray frock,
And sadle your Goate, or your greene Cock,
And make his bridle a bottome of thrid,
To roule up how many miles you have rid.
   Quickly, come away:
   For we, all, stay.

   Nor yet? Nay, then,
   Wee'll try her agen.

3. CHARME.

The Owle is abroad, the Bat, and the Toade,
   And so is the Cat-à-Mountaine;
The Ant, and the Mole sit both in a hole,
   And Frog peepes out o'the fountayne.

(283–285:48–78)

It is not the overt meaning here that is important. The reciting of charms is characteristic of witches, and these lines have the same dramatic validity as the costumes or the anti-masque dances. Jonson is concerned with setting up and describing his figures, not with what they do, but with what they are; for their actions are simply a function of their natures. This idea bears a certain obvious affinity with the concept of a comedy of humors. Though Jonsonian comedy could be a fairly flexible medium, and though there are masques less doctrinaire about the world than *Queenes,* it is nevertheless true that in both forms the basic method is to define the characters and then bring them together: all the action follows logically, and often mechanically, from the dramatis personae. What we must consider in passages like the one above is the way in which the definition is achieved: what is it, exactly, that is being expressed?

For the most part, the verse here is a medium for neither exposition nor dramatic interchange. From the outset, action in the masque — what happens — cannot be expressed through the ordinary means of the stage. The charms are magical, and the poetry itself now has an active function in the dramatic structure of the work. For the witches to speak to each other, their rhetoric must undergo a radical change and take on the regularity of the five-foot couplets examined above or of the quatrains with which, in response to their leader, the hags describe themselves.

Nevertheless, in an important way the charms do express action. We are aware of the amount and kind of physical movement implicit in the rhythmic changes of the verse:

> From the dungeon, from the tree,
> That they die on, here are wee,
> Comes she not yet?
> Strike another heate.

> The Weather is fayre, the wind is good.

The transitions, like the witches' dance, are characterized by abruptness and violence. The rhetoric, too, contributes to a sense of strangeness and disproportion:

> Quickly, come away:
> For we, all, stay.

> Nor yet? Nay, then,
> Wee'll try her agen.

Here the second line has been lengthened by the insertion

of two syntactically unneccessary commas; and the four syllables of the third line require a full stop after the second and a pause after the third. The first and fourth lines, with five syllables each, read much faster (and the quarto and folio speed things up even further by omitting the comma after "Quickly," which appears only in Jonson's manuscript). Lest anyone doubt that the disproportion of the verse is a carefully calculated effect, Jonson has added an explanatory note to the third charm: "All this is but a Periphrasis of the night" (line 80, note K).

In contrast to the antimasque, the masque is all proportion. Its setting is architecture — "a glorious and magnificent Building, figuring the House of Fame" — and from its dances, "if Mathematicians had lost proportion, they might there have found it." The witches talk all the time, in rough rhythmically strong verse; it is the decorum of the queens not to talk at all. Silence, like the age, is golden. Heroic Virtue and Fame speak in couplets, like the witches' Dame, but they adduce a world of certainties and clear values:

> So should, at FAMES loud sound, and VERTUES sight
> All poore, and envious Witchcraft fly the light.
> I did not borrow *Hermes* wings, nor aske
> His crooked sword, nor put on *Pluto's* caske,
> Nor, on mine arme advauncd wise *Pallas* sheild,
> (By which, my face avers'd, in open feild
> I slew the *Gorgon*) for an empty name:
> When *Vertue* cut of *Terror*, he gat *Fame*.
> And, if when *Fame* was gotten, *Terror* dyde
> What black *Erynnis*, or more Hellish pride
> Durst arme these Hagges, now she'is growne, and great,
> To think they could her Glories once defeate?
>
> (302:367–379)

Virtue speaks with that literary self-consciousness peculiar to the masque world: this "Person . . . in the furniture of Perseus" is aware of himself as a figure in an allegory. Indeed, he even allegorizes himself: "When Vertue cut of Terror, he gat Fame." His tone is that of formal oratory; the verse is not dramatic, for drama is by nature dialectical, and Virtue assumes that there can be no alternative to the position he has taken. What he says can, for the most part, be expressed within the bounds of the closed couplet; his rhetoric has both Jacobean heaviness and neoclassic neatness. To observe that it also lacks both Jacobean strength and neoclassic grace may supply us with additional evidence for a point considered in an earlier chapter: it was easier for Jonson to be convincing in his antimasques than in his masques. In contrast to the witches' deviousness, Virtue is perfectly straightforward — and well he may be since, as his opening couplet tells us, he lives in a world where whatever ought to be, is.

If the rhythmic changes of the antimasque incantations left us unsure of what we could rely on, the songs of the masque crystallize the formal order of which the queens' pageant has been an embodiment:

> Helpe, helpe all Tongues, to celebrate this wonder:
> The voyce of FAME should be as loud as Thonder.
>> Her House is all of *echo* made,
>> Where never dies the sound;
>> And, as her browes the cloudes invade,
>> Her feete do strike the ground.
> Sing then *good Fame*, that's out of *Vertue* borne
> For, Who doth fame neglect, doth vertue scorne.
>
> (315:723-730)

This initiates the revels. The opening couplet reaches out to include the audience in the celebration of the triumph of Fame and Virtue; a quatrain describes their ubiquitousness; the whole is resolved in another couplet. The eloquence is formal — as formal, indeed, as the figure of Fame in Cesare Ripa's *Iconologia*, from which Jonson says he took his description. So the values of the masque world are personified in the pageant of queens, represented in the stylized images of Renaissance iconography, and crystallized in song. The stasis of the vision is only emphasized by the curious violence of Jonson's characterization —

> And, as her browes the cloudes invade,
> Her feete do strike the ground.

But Fame is an emblem; Virtue, though armed, has no field for action; the possibility of conflict has been banished with the witches. A second song acclaims, very briefly, the present age and its queen, who is the embodiment of all the virtues of the past. There is nothing left for verse in the masque world but to sing the praises of an achieved ideal, and the only action possible now is defined by the dance.

The final song points a moral for the work:

> Force Greatnesse, all the glorious wayes
>   You can, it soone decayes;
>   But so *good Fame* shall, never:
> Her triumphs, as theyr Causes, are for ever.
>   (316:770–773)

There is much syntactical awkwardness here, as if the poetry of statement were unwillingly contained by an alien, lyric mode. Yet, if we listen, the song has a grace of movement that comes from the subtle variation in the length of lines. As in the antimasque, what we hear through Ferrabosco's music is not the meaning of the words. And there is, then, nothing more to say: "To conclude which, I know no worthyer way of *Epilogue,* then the celebration of Who were the *Celebraters.* The Queenes Majestie . . . etc." (316:774ff).

8. THE ELEMENTS RECONCILED

I have tried to show Jonson dealing with one aspect of the complex problem outlined earlier in these pages. For *The Masque of Queenes* he developed a verse that was expressively adequate for a form he conceived as basically nondramatic. There is still, of course, a great deal of the masque that the verse cannot cope with: I have noted how often the text of *Queenes* resorts to prose descriptions of the action. Significantly enough, too, these are not given as stage directions — that is, as part of the script — but rather as reports of what happened on a particular evening in 1609. They emphasize precisely that quality which Daniel, in his attack on Jonson, had claimed as all-important: the ephemeral and occasional nature of the work.

Oberon, as we have seen, is much more of a whole. Its verse, if less spectacular, is a more satisfactory medium in that it is sufficient for the expression of nearly all the action in the masque. What it cannot handle is the descent from the stage, the transition to the revels: *Oberon* presents a dramatic world of so much definition and consistency that it contains no means of stepping outside itself. The problem is precisely opposite to that of *The Masque of Queenes* — not "what action can culminate in these revels?" but "what place can there be for the revels in this action?" A satisfactory solution requires a masque world that the masquers can move beyond without destroying. By 1618 Jonson had found such a solution.

I have said that one way of viewing the central action of the masque is as a conflict between two kinds of dancing; and in a sense the poet's and the architect's fight ignored one really basic element of the form, the revels. Every one of my examinations of a Jonsonian masque has ultimately returned to the problem of the court dances and to Jonson's comparative success or failure to see this problem in literary terms. Otto Gombosi argues from the continuing concern of masque writers with the revels that the literary aspects of the masque may be largely ignored: "By virtue of its origin the masque was, in the first place, dance, and naturally, dance music — and by virtue of its history, in the second place, spectacular entertainment. Only in the third place was the masque literature, whereby the song-text, with its music, easily maintained a certain degree of preponderance over monologue and dialogue." [13] Gombosi takes the antimasque to be "obvious additions to the core" of the masque and continues, "The masque as a literary form is amorphous; as a form of choreographic entertainment, it is highly organized. Dance gives the masque its form."

We may fairly question the validity of an argument that the masque is essentially choreographic because its origin lies in dance. In the first place, we have seen that the tradition of mumming is as important in the development of the masque as the revels; and in the second place, the dialogue that was so insignificant in 1501 at the wedding of Katherine of Aragon had, by 1516, taken the form of indispensable explanatory "spechys after the devys of Mr. Kornyche." As soon as we have found dialogue to be essential to an understanding of the action, we have acknowledged, simply, that dialogue *has* become essential. As to the point about the antimasque, it is perhaps vain to wonder what the core was to which King Edward's masques "of apes and bagpipes, of cats, of Greek worthies, and of 'medyoxes' " were obvious additions. But we may wish to recall that the whole concept of misrule is so central to the revels that Henry VIII's early masques (which often employed the sudden appearance of the king and courtiers, fantastically dressed, to interrupt a banquet) bear as many earmarks of the antimasque as of the masque.

The real point is that all three elements, choreographic, theatrical, and literary, are equally basic to the developing form. We must beware of a historical argument that confuses "rudimentary" with "basic." Granted that the masque, even as Jonson conceived it, was built around prepared and traditional dances; we must at the same time ask ourselves how much structural use Jonson was able to make of them. In terms of the action of the masque, the point made by the revels is that the masquers are capable of moving from the stage into the world of the court. The dancing itself serves as an interruption, especially if (as in most of the later masques) the action continues after the revels. In 1527, Crane in *Riches and Love* had conceived of dance as integral to his work in such a way that the choreography became instrumental in concluding the masque. But for Jonson, who merged the three aspects of the Tudor form — dialogue, spectacle, dance — into one literary text, it was the *idea* of the revels that was significant. We find him minimizing their traditional importance by letting poetry usurp the function of dance as the conclusion of the work, and so pushing the revels further and further back toward the middle of the masque. Perhaps he even attempted to cut down the time given over to dancing. We know, at any rate, that one viewer in 1618, dissatisfied and without the prerogative of asking for his money back, complained loudly that the revels were too short.

The changes Jonson effected in the form were largely changes in emphasis, but we should not underestimate their importance. If the masque in the sixteenth century was essentially choreographic (and even this seems to me an overstatement of the case), it was no longer so in Jonson's hands. He conceived the form anew and educated his audience to appreciate it. To demonstrate this, it is only necessary to recall the contemporary attacks on the production of 1618: "The conceit good," wrote Sir Edward Harwood, "the poetry not so." Nathaniel Brent thought that "the poet is growen so dull that his devise is not worth the relating, much less the copying out." [14] Whatever the quality of the perception, the terms are those of literary criticism. When spectators begin viewing masques as poetic texts, we no longer have any justification for not considering the form as literature. We may see the process of change fairly well completed by 1618, in *Pleasure Reconcild to Vertue*.

Orazio Busino, chaplain to the Venetian embassy in London, describes the opening of the masque as follows:

The Lord Chamberlain . . . had the way cleared and in the middle of the theatre there appeared a fine and spacious area carpeted all over with green cloth. In an instant a large curtain dropped, painted to represent a tent of gold cloth with a broad fringe; the background was of canvas painted blue, powdered all over with golden stars. This became the front arch of the stage, forming a drop scene, and on its being removed there appeared first of all Mount Atlas, whose enormous head alone was visible up aloft under the very roof of the theatre; it rolled up its eyes and moved itself very cleverly. [15]

Jonson tells us nothing of this front curtain, and it does not appear to have been especially germane to the text: the tent does not, presumably, contain Mount Atlas. But as we read further in Busino's letter, we come upon several other things he saw of which the poet makes no mention — a pantomime battle between Hercules and Antaeus, for example, and the reappearance of the goddess Virtue when Daedalus enters. Indeed, far from being the record of a particular production on a particular evening in 1618, the text seems almost to testify to the irrelevance of the spectator's experience. Davison's *Masque of Proteus* has a certain viability as a historical document, to which its aesthetic qualities are merely incidental. *The Masque of Queenes* justifies its existence on artistic grounds to a greater extent than *Proteus* does. Nevertheless, there is, as we have seen, much of the character of a

W HEN HERCVLES, was dowtfull of his waie,
  Inclofed rounde, with vertue, and with vice:
With reafons firfte, did vertue him affaie,
The other, did with pleafures him entice:
  They longe did ftriue, before he coulde be wonne,
  Till at the lengthe, ALCIDES thus begonne.

Oh pleafure, thoughe thie waie bee fmoothe, and faire,
And fweete delightes in all thy courtes abounde:
Yet can I heare, of none that haue bene there,
That after life, with fame haue bene renoumde:
  For honor hates, with pleafure to remaine,
  Then houlde thy peace, thow waftes thie winde in vaine.

But heare, I yeelde oh vertue to thie will,
And vowe my felfe, all labour to indure,
For to afcende the fteepe, and craggie hill,
The toppe whereof, whoe fo attaines, is fure
  For his rewarde, to haue a crowne of fame:
  Thus HERCVLES, obey'd this facred dame.

Virgil. in Fragm. de littera y.
Quifquis enim duros cafus virtutis amore Vicerit, ille fibi laudémque decúfque parabit.
At qui defidiâ luxúmque fequetur inertem, Dum fugit oppofitos incauta mente labores, Turpis, inépfque fimul, miferabile tranfiget æuum.

Pœna

Figure 1. Hercules' meeting with Virtue and Vice

Figure 2. Comus

Le masque est bienseant à l'ame desguisée,
Et la danse & le bal conuient à l'inconstant,
L'un cache son dessein, & voile sa pensée,
Et l'autre nous fait voir qu'il n'est iamais contant:

Comme on voit ce flambeau se consommer soy-mesme,
Et ces chappeaux de fleurs deçà delà iettez;
Tout ainsi fait COMVS à celuy là qu'il aime,
Car il se perd en fin dedans les voluptez.

Figure 3. Comus and revelers

EMBLEMA

SINE CERERE ET BACCHO
friget venus.

Ἄλογα *habent certas potandi animantia leges,*
Vltra demenſum bellua nulla bibit:
Nos homines autem recta ratione vigentes,
Nos madidus Iacchus nocte dieq; rigat.

In

Figure 4.   Burghers at revels

souvenir program about our text of the 1609 masque, and it is a character that Jonson is at some pains to maintain. But *Pleasure Reconcild to Vertue* is very nearly self-sufficient as a work of literature. Even its dances become poetry.

For the protagonist of his masque, Jonson uses Hercules, who, as Hallett Smith writes, "to the sixteenth century . . . was a moral hero, a champion against tyranny, and a model for any young aristocrat to follow. For the Renaissance stressed, not the twelve labors or the other feats familiar to us, but a legend in which the hero is shown deliberately choosing the kind of life he will lead." [16] The legend behind the masque title is explicitly referred to only late in the work (lines 257–260). First recounted by Xenophon,[17] it was extremely popular and, by the time of the Renaissance, was considered the most significant part of the story of Hercules.

As a fable illustrating the moral life, Hercules' choice was naturally employed by a number of compilers of emblem books. To Geoffrey Whitney, *"Bivium virtutis et vitii"* is not the crossroad depicted in most of his continental models, but a dramatic encounter, literally a "scene"; for the hero's meeting with Virtue and Vice takes place not in a landscape but on a stage with a Serlian street as its setting (see Figure 1).[18] Whitney exemplifies the tendency of the Elizabethan moralist, with his puritan background, to intensify the issue, to make of the ethical conflict a formal debate, and to see in the active hero a rational soul subject to persuasion. We learn something from the emblem tradition that we cannot learn from all the didacticism of the *Masque of Queenes*: that moral alternatives are significant only insofar as they relate to the human will and represent voluntary commitments. It was not until 1634 that a poet (who had certainly read *Pleasure Reconcild to Vertue*) was to conceive of a masque not as a court ballet, but as a drama about the will. That "Maske presented at Ludlow Castle" has been so consistently misinterpreted that, since the eighteenth century, it has masqueraded under the name of its villain, the leader of its anti-masque. The modern title, *Comus*, is grossly unjust to the work: we would not think of referring to *Paradise Lost* as *Satan*.

Hercules has made his choice between Virtue and Pleasure long before the opening of Jonson's masque. (It is of course only the enemies of Pleasure who would call her "Vice"; the two names are, however, synonymous to most writers, including Whitney.) The title proclaims it a drama not of opposition but of reconciliation: the masque, as always, has as its function the resolution of all conflict. Yet the basic opposition of the title is closer to Jonson's idea of what a masque should be than we may realize. We have already looked briefly at contemporary attitudes toward these court productions: dismissive remarks range from the indulgent warnings of Bacon ("These Things are but Toyes . . .") who approved, on the whole, of masque dancing,[19] but thought figure dances were "a childish curiosity," to the sort of outright attack of which Jonson himself gives us a good example in the antimasque of *Love Restored*. In order to answer the puritan charges within that masque, it is only necessary to unmask Plutus and reveal him as a hypocrite. A less summary treatment is required in the larger world outside: while the moral grounds of the puritan position toward the revels may be untenable, a glance at the exchequer records for James I's reign will convince us that on economic grounds the position is a strong one. Critics have complained of Milton's sourness in making Comus his villain; but the god of revelry is a god of excesses, who must be banished from Jonson's world too before the reconciliation of pleasure and virtue can be effected.

Milton's Comus is a forceful rhetorician and a first-rate poet. Indeed, in 1939 he was able to persuade as staunch a partisan of virtue as Douglas Bush that "one would rather live with Comus than with the Lady." [20] By 1945, the same critic had somewhat reduced his adversary's stature: "Comus is, in fact," he writes, "a cultured gentleman, a cavalier poet." [21] We may not, I think, be mistaken if we detect a little bravado in that "in fact"; Milton, like Plato, realized precisely how attractive evil had to be to deceive us into thinking it good. Few of us will leave cavalier poetry with much regret; Comus' verse — as Bush himself remarks — is Shakespearean.

One must have taste to admire the Comus of 1634. It is not the Lady, however, but we ourselves who must learn to perceive the distinction between aesthetics and morality, and who come away with a lesson for our lives. The audience at Ludlow Castle was being taught to mistrust appearances. In contrast, the spectators at Whitehall in 1618 had more faith that the aesthetic judgment was the right one. Merely by looking at Jonson's Comus, they knew who and what he was. The god who opens *Pleasure Reconcild to Vertue* is himself a stock character of comedy: the souse, the fat man, pure sensual appetite. Shakespeare's version of him is Falstaff, another god of comedy who must be banished before the accession of virtue. And yet the figure, traditional enough in its way, is by no means the traditional Comus.

Philostratus, whose *Imagines* Jonson often used as a source for details about the appearance of mythological figures, describes "the spirit Comus, to whom men owe their revelling" as "a youth . . . delicate and not yet full grown, flushed with wine and, though erect . . . asleep under the influence of drink." He holds a torch, flame downward, and "the torch seems to be falling from his right hand as sleep relaxes it." He is "stationed at the doors of a chamber," the time is night, and a "very wealthy pair, just married . . . are lying on a couch."

And what else is there of the revel? Well, what but the revellers? Do you not hear the castanets and the flute's shrill note and the disorderly singing? The torches give a faint light, enough for the revellers to see what is close in front of them, but not enough for us to see them. Peals of laughter rise, and women rush along with men, wearing men's sandals and garments girt in strange fashion; for the revel permits women to masquerade as men, and men to put on women's garb and to ape the walk of women. Their crowns are no longer fresh but, crushed down on the head on account of the wild running of the dancers, they have lost their joyous look.[22]

Vincenzo Cartari, depicting the pagan gods for the Renaissance, summarizes Philostratus' description, but only partially follows it in his illustration of the god (see Figure 2).[23] Comus stands before a closed door, in broad daylight now, though still holding his drooping torch. As in Italian Renaissance paintings, the indoor scene is almost outdoors — we can see hills and sky through the large window — and the room is one side of a stage set, half a box from which the front wall has been removed. On the floor lie flowers; but the "wealthy pair, just married" and the revelers are nowhere to be seen. They are behind the closed door, and their revelry is now wholly embodied in the single symbolic figure who stands outside it.

A French artist named Jasper Isaac in 1613 went a step further (see Figure 3). For a French translation of Philostratus [24] he prepared an engraving depicting Comus in a scene with a certain contemporary relevance. The figure of the god (clearly adapted from Cartari, since it includes details from his illustration, but omits several from the original description) stands at the very front of the scene, torch and spear in hand. He is before the door of a chamber, but now the door is open, and its huge arch has become a proscenium framing everything except Comus himself. We are looking into a large hall lighted by candles whose feverish brightness is emphasized by the rays surrounding them. Directly before us a masque dance is in progress; the revelers, five women and another Comus, are dressed in classical costume. In the middle of the room to the right stand spectators and three more ladies waiting to dance, in poses reminiscent of the classical Graces. Above them sit the musicians. An accompanying poem interprets the significance of the dance:

> Le masque est bien seant à l'ame desguisée,
> Et la danse et le bal convient à l'inconstant,
> L'un cache son dessein, et voile sa pensée,
> Et l'autre nous fait voir qu'il n'est jamais contant:
> Comme on voit ce flambeau se consommer soy-mesme,
> Et ces chappeaux de fleurs deçà delà jettez;
> Tout ainsi fait Comus à celui là qu'il aime;
> Car il se perd en fin dedans les voluptez.

(The mask is quite fitting for the disguised soul, and dances and balls are appropriate to the inconstant man: the former hides his intentions and veils his thoughts; the latter lets us see that he is never satisfied. Just as we see this torch burning itself out, and these chaplets of flowers strewn in every direction, even so does Comus treat his favorite, who is ruined amidst his pleasures.)

The poem describes a heavily moralized emblematic scene, which is not entirely depicted in the engraving. The dancers, for example, are meant to be masked; but the artist, presumably to stress the misery of the chronic reveler's life, has left their faces bare. Their expressions, like that of their patron, show weariness: this is the awful fate of the debauchee who finds he is not really happy but cannot think of anything else to do. Curiously enough, the masque dance, which Jonson allowed to symbolize the harmony and permanence of an ideal world, is here the precinct of that archvillain Inconstancy, patron of the antimasque.

To the left of the dancing, a banquet is under way. Isaac has taken his cue from Cartari, who compares the spirit of revelry with Bacchus and observes that "Como . . . fu appresso de gli antichi il Dio de i convivi" [25] — the ancients considered Comus the god of banquets. We can perceive the figure undergoing a curious transformation here. Philostratus never mentions that Comus presides at feasts, but stresses his involvement with love, wine, and dance; and Philostratus is the ancient whom Cartari explicitly cites as his source. In sixteenth-century Italy, a revel presumably included dinner; nevertheless, even to Cartari Comus was not a god of excess. The "convivi" carry no overtones of gluttony here; they are the banquets of Dante's *Convito* and Plato's *Symposium*. Indeed, votaries of the god are committed to taking even their liquor in moderation:

egli era giovine, allegro e giocondo: perche beendo gli huomini temperatemente svegliano gli spiriti, e piu arditi diventano, e piu lieti, e sono etiando creduti essere di migliore ingegno allhora.[26]
(He [Comus] was young, cheerful and merry: because when men drink temperately, their spirits are aroused, and become more bold and more happy; and they are then even considered to be more talented.)

Cartari emphasizes temperance, high spirits, *ingegno* — wit, intelligence, ability, primarily intellectual qualities. But by 1613, Jasper Isaac understood revelry to include *gourmandise,* and thus the French artist represents Comus' masque as the proper entertainment at a lavish feast. Twenty-one years later, Milton's Lady was to refuse indignantly the offer of a drink and to charge Comus with promoting "swinish gluttony." [27]

None of Isaac's diners, however, shows the slightest interest in the courtly dance, and the exoticism of their dress gives us a clue to the moral of the picture. The masquers are in classical costume; masquing is a pagan pursuit. But the feasters are clothed after the Eastern style; they wear turbans and rich flowing robes. They are luxurious Orientals, heathens — gluttony is one of the seven deadly sins — and the whole is an emblem admonishing the Christian soul. Indeed, the engraver has personified his admonition in two figures. At the front of the audience stand an elderly bearded man and his companion, the latter clearly in ecclesiastical dress. Both are raising their hands, evidently deploring the scene.

Before returning to Jonson, we may pursue the iconography of the revels a little further. An emblem book by Heinrich Assenheim, published at Frankfurt in 1619,[28] displays a rather less elegant banquet, with a less complex moral from the *Adagia* of Erasmus: "Without Ceres and Bacchus, Venus grows cold" (see Figure 4). There is, however, an abundance of all three in the illustration. Assenheim may never have seen a copy of either Philostratus or Cartari; nevertheless, his "moral hieroglyphic" provides a striking contrast to the scene depicted by Jasper Isaac. Unlike his French contemporary, for whom the dangers of sensual pleasure were represented by exoticism, the German engraver brings his food, liquor, and sex very much down to earth. These are burghers, and they are, literally, making pigs out of themselves. The verse moralizes on drinking:

> *Aloga* habent certas potandi animantia leges,
> Ultra demensum bellua nulla bibit:
> Nos homines autem recta ratione vigentes,
> Nos madidus Iacchus nocte dieque rigat.

(Unreasoning creatures have fixed laws of drinking. No beast drinks intemperately. We men, however, flourishing in right reason — dripping Iacchus [Bacchus] moistens us night and day.)

We must, presumably, omit pigs from the class of beasts that know when to stop drinking ("The pig," it is said, "is rightly so named"); otherwise there would seem to be little point in the transformation. But there is more than a feast here; there is dancing too. Though it is less formal than the French masque, the revels have their leader. Comus, who in France was described as bringing his devotees to perdition, in Germany six years later is iconographically replaced by death. He leads the dance, with his predecessor's spear in one hand and, in the other, a less adequate though more universal symbol of dissolution than Comus' inverted torch, an hourglass. The devil — a horned beast — provides the music. A second death figure, also bearing arms and time, enters through a rear window, as if to surround the company with the moral of the emblem.

The Comus who opens *Pleasure Reconcild to Vertue* bears little resemblance to the youth of Philostratus on whose image we have seen so many changes wrought. The provenance of Jonson's figure is suggested by Allen H. Gilbert, who cites a classical representation of Silenus, participating in a bacchic rout.[29] Yet even here Jonson will not be limited by his sources; the Silenus of *Oberon* possessed "all gravitie, and profound knowledge" and could lead his satyrs toward moderation and virtue. The poet's sense of his characters is essentially dramatic, not conventional, and we need not search out Isaac Casaubon's gems to see the figure for ourselves. We need only attend to the opening of the masque:

To a wild Musique of *Cimbals Flutes*, & *Tabers*, is brought forth Comus, the god of *Cheere*, or the *belly*, riding in tryumph, . . . his haire curld: They that wayt upon him, crownd with Ivy, their Javelyns don about with it: one of them going with Hercules *Bowle* bare before him: while the rest present him, with this

Song.
Roome, roome, make roome for the bouncing belly,
first father of Sauce, & deviser of gelly,
Prime master of arts, & the giver of wit,
That found out the excellent ingine, the spit.   (479:4–16)

The contemporary audience found itself at once in a very familiar world of misrule, for the mummers traditionally opened their plays with a vociferous demand for room in which to perform. We, on the other hand, may find in this only an amusing indication of what Jonson's idea of revelry was. Philostratus' patron of dancing, wine, and love has been transformed into "the god of Cheere, or the belly"; and our Venetian observer Busino, logically enough, thought he was seeing "a very chubby Bacchus."[30] There are, however, reasons for the change that are more integral to the masque form. Dancing, after all, represents a value that the work is ultimately to assert, so the villain cannot very well be the god of dance. The sort of pleasure that Hercules must banish because it is inconsistent with virtue is purely sensual pleasure, which has no higher aim than the gratification of appetite. This is what Jonson's Comus stands for, though the lusty verse of the opening song makes considerable claims for its subject. "Prime master of arts" he is called, and a list of his inventions follows. To be fair to an underdog, it is an impressive list, though perhaps lacking in variety:

> the spit,
> the plough, & the flaile, the mill, & the Hoppar,
> the hutch, & the bowlter, the furnace, & coppar,
> the Oven, the bavin, the mawkin, & peele
> the harth, & the range, the dog, & the wheele.
> He, he first invented both hogshead & Tun,
> the gimblet, & vice too; & taught 'em to run.
>
> (480:17–22)

The verse in which the god is celebrated is not subtly orchestrated; it is heavily rhythmical, and we hear in it the percussive beat of the cymbals and tabors more than the melody of the flutes. As we read, too, we easily tire of the sameness of the rhythmic pattern. By the end of the song it becomes apparent that, if appetite is a source of invention, it needs a good deal of control to remain creative — control which, as the song makes clear in a final play on words, the god has lost and which the verse itself has barely maintained:

> All which have now made thee, so wide i' the waste
> as scarce with no pudding thou art to be lac'd:
> but eating & drincking, untill thou dost nod
> thou break'st all thy girdles, & breakst forth a god.
>
> (480:33–36)

A figure bearing the great drinking bowl of Hercules now interrupts, and the masque becomes prose. His harangue undercuts both the song and the figure it has celebrated:

Now you sing of god Comus here, the *Belly-god*. I say it is well, & I say it is not well: it is well, as it is a Ballad, and the Belly worthie of it I must say, and 'twer forty yards of ballad, more: as much ballad as tripe: but when the Belly is not edified by it, it is not well: for where did you ever read, or heare, that the Belly had any eares? Come, never pump for an answeare, for you are defeated.   (481:44–51)

What he is saying is that Comus has become appetite without intelligence. In a work that is to be about wisdom, the bowl-bearer points out at once how far the "giver of wit" is even from sense. His prose should save us from too uncritical an admiration for the energy of the opening scene; he himself, however, is obviously not a disapproving critic. Busino describes him as "a stout individual on foot, dressed in red short clothes, who made a speech, reeling about like a drunkard, tankard in hand." Our observer found his scene "very gay and burlesque." As the bowl-bearer continues, he becomes, suitably enough, a master of ceremonies for the first antimasque, ordering its dancers onto the stage:

I would have a *Tun* now, brought in to daunce, and so many *Bottles* about it: Ha? you looke as if you would make a probleme of this: do you see? a problem? why *Bottles*? and why a *Tun*? and why a *Tun*, and why *Bottles*? to daunce? I say, that men that drink hard, and serve the belly in any place of quality (as the *Joviall Tinkers*, or a *lusty kindred*) are living measures of drinck: and can transforme themselves, & doe every daie, to *Bottles* or *Tuns* when they please.   (481–482:68–76)

The first antimasque dance follows, "danced by Men in the shape of bottles, tuns, &c." They were, reports Busino, "twelve extravagant masquers, one of whom was in a barrel, all but his extremities, his companions being similarly cased in huge wicker flasks, very well made. They danced awhile to the sound of the cornets and trumpets, performing various and most extravagant antics."

This antimasque presents figures who have ceased to be

men and who have become mere containers for what will
satisfy their appetites, "living measures of drinck." They are
creatures of the earth, without mind or spirit. Fittingly, it is
at this point that Hercules enters to engage Antaeus, the son
of Earth, in pantomime battle. Busino, our only source for
the scene (though the text does imply, at line 88, that it took
place), says that it was played after the end of the dance:
"These [dancers] were followed by a gigantic man representing Hercules with his club, who strove with Antaeus and
performed other feats." Clearly, however, it is the hero's
speech, not the fight, that brings the revelry to a halt.[31]

With the appearance of the hero, the verse takes on a control that is able to impose order on the chaos of the antimasque. The near doggerel of the opening song, and the
bowl-bearer's prose, is banished by Jonsonian couplets:

> What rytes are theis? breeds Earth more Monsters yet?
> *Antaeus* scarce is cold: what can beget
> this store? (& stay) such contraries upon her?
> Is Earth so fruitfull of hir owne dishonor?
> Or 'cause his vice was Inhumanitie
> hopes she, with vitious hospitalitie
> to work an expiation first? and then
> (help Vertue) theis are Sponges, & not men.
> Bottles? meere vessells? half a tun of panch?
> how? & the other half thrust forth in hanch?
> Whose *Feast*? the Bellies? *Comus*? and my Cup
> brought in to fill the druncken *Orgies* up?   (482:87–98)

The first part of the speech continually reverts to expletives
and exclamatory words and phrases: "what can beget / this
store? (& stay) such contraries upon her?" ("and stay" is an
expression of surprise, and the last phrase is part of a sentence reading, "What can beget such contraries upon her?").
Or again, "(help Vertue) theis are Sponges, & not men," or
"Bottles? meere vessells? half a tun of panch? / how?" or
"Whose Feast? the Bellies? Comus?"

But as Hercules' anger abates and his mind moves toward

the action that is his responsibility, the verse takes on a
dignity and directness new to the masque:

> Burdens, & shames of nature, perish, dye,
> for yet you never liv'd; But in the stye
> of vice have wallow'd; & in that Swines strife
> byn buried under the offence of life.
>
> (482-483:101-104)

The masque is beginning to put the pleasures of Comus in
their proper place, to imply that there are higher pleasures
than those of either burlesque or appetite — for example,
"the crownd reward / of thirstie *Heröes* after labour hard"
(482:99-100) — and to stress the responsibilities of being
human, the acceptance of which constitutes virtue. It is precisely the movement of this speech that lets us know we are
leaving the disorder of the antimasque behind and shows us,
through the gesture with which Hercules concludes, the
figure who makes the transition possible.

The hero takes the dances he has encountered for a religious ceremony; it is, in fact, a Dionysiac revel. As he describes
it, it also becomes a kind of grotesque fertility rite: "breeds
Earth more Monsters yet?" he asks. The antimasque appears
to him an inversion of the order of nature, and ultimately
through his speech we see that the scenes which Busino found
so "very gay and burlesque" have all the characteristics of the
witches' antimasque in *The Masque of Queenes*. Like the
"ougly Hell" of 1609, the ivy grove of Comus is insupport-
able once Virtue has made its appearance on the scene; and
the grove too will vanish, with the god, into the machine Inigo
Jones has provided. But here the victory has been accomplished in more human terms. Victory is perhaps the
wrong word; the only *battle* Hercules wins in the antimasque
is one Jonson has seen fit to omit from his text. The hero is
a figure who can enter the world of misrule, assess it, and
lead us from it into the masque.

There has been no dramatic conflict between vice and vir-

CONCILED

tue here. What a spectator has witnessed up to this point is two scenes of music and dance, with interludes of commentary on them. Speeches are not exchanged between the characters, but made to a general audience. The example of *Oberon* has been examined and its dangers avoided. Hercules' world is not the world of drama, but a less fully detailed and more clearly allegorical one; though the kind of action the hero performs would be totally inadequate as part of a dramatic conflict, it provides here the crucial transitions of the masque. Thus the metamorphosis of the offending landscape is effected simply by the presence of active virtue. Hercules concludes, with true Jonsonian authority,

> Theis *Monsters* plague themselves: & fitly too,
> for they do suffer what, and all they doo.
> But here must be no shelter, nor no shrowd
> for such: Sinck *Grove,* or vanish into clowd.
>
> (483:111–114)

And so it happens: "After this, the whole *Grove* vanisheth, and the whole *Musique* is discovered, sitting at the foote of the *Mountaine,* with *Pleasure* & *Virtue* seated above them" (483:115–118). The hero has already implied that there are higher pleasures than those Comus offers. We see, as the new scene appears, that Pleasure has not been banished from the masque, but sits at the side of Virtue in an emblematic assurance of the reconciliation promised by the title.

This masque has been so constructed that it can expose its machinery in a way which would have constituted a structural threat to either *The Masque of Queenes* or *Oberon.* The former presents a world limited by alternatives so rigidly defined that there can be no transition from one to the other; and the latter is primarily concerned with maintaining the consistency of its dramatic illusion. Hercules commands a change of scene here, and the change is accomplished with something like the mysterious "sodayne . . . sound of loud Musique" [32] that had accompanied the harrowing of hell nine years before. But now, as the scene opens, part of what we discover is "the whole Musique." The point is that the work now acknowledges, as its masque landscape appears, that music is integral to the form — and if to the form, then to the scene also. Music is what turns verse to song and song to dance; it is the groundwork of the revels; and this is the masque above all others in which Jonson has made the revels integral to his text.

So the transformation scene opens with a song: "The *Quire* invyte *Hercules* to rest." What follows is the first lyric verse in the masque:

> Great frend, and servant of the good,
> let coole a while thy heated blood,
> and from thy mightie labor cease.
>   Lye downe, lye downe,
> and give thy trobled spirits peace,
>   whilst Vertue, for whose sake
> thou dost this god-like travaile take,
> may of the choicest herbage make,
>   upon this Mountaine bred,
>   a Crowne, a Crowne
>   for thy immortall head.   (483:120–130)

In terms of the action, the song urges the hero to change from the scourge of the antimasque to our guide into the masque. It also lets us know that we no longer have our feet on the ground, so to speak; for only the antimasque is required to maintain the illusion of being a world like our own — the illusion, that is, of drama. Its changes, like ours, are the result of mutability, the accidents of time. The masque, on the other hand, uncovers its machinery and claims that its metamorphoses are only representations of the way things really happen. What it shows us are not characters — whereas even the antimasque's bowl-bearer, brief as his part is, has a personality — but figures who (like Oberon) may also take on symbolic value. Its gestures are made through the medium of dance; and its values are defined by song.

But the transition to the masque is not instantaneous. The hero slumbers, and for a few moments we are in a sort of limbo between the worlds of mutability and metamorphosis. The song that sets the scene has the virtues of simplicity and directness, but it does little toward providing us with an alternative to the vitality of the antimasque. The reward it offers for labor is merely rest, though it holds out the promise of something greater. There is, in fact, relatively little for the lyric to do in this world as yet. We require more exposition — indeed, we hardly know where we are — and it is precisely the crystallization of what we have *already* perceived that the superb concluding masque songs will offer us.

The choir has stressed virtue as the source of Hercules' action, but it has stressed "travaile" too. Virtue, we conclude, must be continually active. At once we have the moral of the song played out on stage before us: "Here *Hercules* being laid downe at their feet; the 2. ANTIMASQUE which is of *Pigmees* appeeres" (484:132–134). The world of the antimasque has an earthly solidness that can be banished by an agent who realizes the superiority of spiritual and moral values. The world of the masque, on the contrary, has so little solidity that it appears to be a state of the hero's mind. Despite Inigo Jones's machine, the consort of musicians, and the presence of the goddesses Pleasure and Virtue, as soon as the hero is no longer on guard, antimasquers can once again invade the scene.

Jonson's source for the story of Hercules' encounter with the pygmies, Philostratus, explains that they "claim to be brothers of Antaeus," earth-born like him, and come to avenge his death.[33] Jonson makes very little of the reason for their appearance on the scene. One pygmy refers briefly to the "murder of our Brother" (line 138), but we are expected to know already that they, like the dancers of the first antimasque, are "contraries" begotten on earth. At least one spectator missed the point: Busino thought he was seeing "twelve masked boys in the guise of frogs." [34] A reader, of course, is in little danger of such confusion; and even if he lacks a classical education, he will catch the familial reference to Antaeus that a listener might miss. It may require a certain subtlety to deduce from their brother's provenance the fact that the pygmies too are earth-born, and from this to perceive that there is a real and rational connection between the first and second antimasques. If so, it is a subtlety Jonson expects only of his readers, for he offers the unlearned spectator hardly a hint.

As the pygmies attack, however, it becomes perfectly clear to the dullest member of the audience that this is a second antimasque. The scene is, in its way, a masterpiece; and in fourteen lines Jonson again brings the resources of drama into battle with the world of the masque. The section is worth quoting in full:

1. Pigmee.
Antaeus dead? and *Hercules* yet live?
Where is this *Hercules*? What wold I give
to meet him, now? meet him? nay, three such other,
if they had hand in murder of our Brother?
With three? with fowre? with ten? nay, with as many
as the *Name* yeilds: pray Anger there be any
whereon to feed my just revenge, and soone,
how shall I kill him? hurle him 'gainst the Moone,
& break him in small portions? give to *Greece*
his braine, & every tract of earth a peece?
2. *Pig.* He is yonder.
1. Where?
3. At the hill foote; a sleep.
1. Let one goe steale his Club.
2. My charge: ile creep.
4. He is ours.
1. Yes: peace.

3. Triumph: we have him, Boy.
4. Sure; sure: he is sure.
1. Come; let us daunce for joy.   (484:134–154)

The stridency of the first pygmy's boasting is emphasized by a rapid series of rising inflections: every sentence in the passage is a question; every full stop requires a rise in the tone of voice. (The folio text significantly replaces the colon after "yeilds" [line 140] with a question mark.) This device is perhaps directed more toward a listener than a reader. The reader, on the other hand, will be aware of the pygmy's frequent short expostulations, breaking the movement of the verse in much the same way as Hercules' expletives and angry queries had interrupted his first speech. But there is a difference. Hercules' exclamations provide occasional breaks in a passage where the direction nevertheless remains clear. His expletives express an anger that precedes (and threatens) both the orderly progress of his verse and the dutiful and rational exertion that constitutes virtue. What follows is the controlled couplets of the latter half of the speech, and we perceive in Hercules' whole passage a development that can logically culminate in positive action — in the gesture that banishes the first antimasque. Hercules appeals to "Vertue," the pygmy to "Anger." The pygmy's speech expresses a chaos that only increases as he continues. The movement from beginning to end is broken by full stops, for the most part in places having nothing to do with the order provided by the verse, and the couplets read like prose. And whereas Hercules' speech gains increasing control through the changing movement of the verse, the pygmy's passage is constructed so that it can have no culmination except an interruption. The pygmy's boasting leads nowhere; it simply goes on and on in a potentially infinite progression of fantasies.

By being readers and not auditors we are able to perceive the conflict between the poetic form of the speech and the prose rhythm behind it. Few of the viewers could have realized that the scene was in verse. And indeed, even the printed text helps to conceal the fact: the folio, followed by all modern editors, prints the pygmies' ensuing dialogue, which comprises four lines of uneven couplets, as if it were ten lines of prose.

The second pygmy interrupts his companion's fulminations, and in the brief, tense, and whispered exchanges that follow, the form of the verse is reasserted to close the scene. The movement of the lines is still irregular; nevertheless the rhyme words are emphasized because they now fall at the ends of sentences, and the return to the couplet provides an organization, however rough, for the rhetoric of the antimasque. The rhythm now gives a positive energy and a new direction to the scene as the pygmies prepare to conclude their dialogue with action: "They Daunce: at the end whereof they think to surprize" the sleeping Hercules.

But the triumph is premature. The choir sings out; the hero "sodainely, being wak'd by the *Musique*, and rowsing himself, they [the pygmies] all all run into holes" (lines 155–158). Busino says that the attackers "were driven off by Hercules." [35] Jonson, however, clearly implies that the pygmies are routed without even a gesture from the hero. This is evident from the "Musique" that wakes him — not the music of the pygmies' dance, which has already stopped, but the choir's song:

> Wake, Hercules, awake: but heave up thy black ey,
> 'tis only ask'd from thee, to looke, & theis wil dy,
> or flie.
> Already they are fled,
> whom scorne had els left dead.   (485:160–164)

Although antimasquers can enter this landscape, we are still very much in a world where the laws of masque apply. When the sleeping hero is endangered, there is a mechanism — indeed, a "whole Musique . . . sitting at the foote of the

Mountaine" — to rouse him. "'Tis only ask'd from thee
to looke," they sing; it is virtue's mere return to conscious-
ness that the antimasquers cannot endure. Just as the commitment to virtue (or to vice) is a consciously willed one,
so even the virtuous mind, the masque says, must be continually watchful against the encroachments of sensuality
and unreason. The position is the strongly humanist one
asserted by Jonson in his moral poetry as well: it is reason that
makes us men, and salvation is achieved not through the body
and blood of Christ, but through conscious adherence to
virtue.[36] The antimasquers have given up their minds for the
indulgence of their senses in the first case and of their pas-
sions in the second. We may perceive from this alone how
much more Milton's masque about the will owes to *Pleasure
Reconcild to Vertue* than the fact that Comus is its villain.

Jonson has made his point; there is no danger that conflict
will again invade the stage, and the main masque can begin.
Now "Mercury descendeth from the Hill" and addresses
Hercules in the oratorical tones that seem to characterize
all exposition in the masque world: "Rest still, thou active
frend of Vertue" (line 168). The adjective should give us a
moment's pause. The hero's activity, except for a fight that
has been excised (deliberately, it begins to appear) from our
text, is wholly mental.[37] The two antimasque episodes tell
us that a virtuous and constant mind will triumph over the
forces of passion. The masque now shows us the mind as it
turns from conflict to the pursuit of wisdom.

"The words of Mercury," Shakespeare tells us, "are harsh
after the songs of Apollo." Here, properly, the Olympian
messenger speaks first. He is a god of prose, or at least of
exposition: the function of messengers is to tell us things
we do not know or, in theatrical terms, to report action that
cannot be represented. We must wait for the god with the
lyre, who will order and relate things we have already perceived, organizing them into a new experience.

It is only partly a paradox to say that the prose of the masque world is the couplet. Even matter as utilitarian as information falls into Jonson's favorite form. Mercury has been sent by Atlas to crown Hercules and lead him to the ultimate reward implied in the masque's title. On the way, the messenger summarizes the history of the hero's relationship with the god who bears the sky on his shoulders. The summary is an extremely scholarly one: Mercury has evidently studied Diodorus on the question of what gift Hercules actually received for rescuing the Hesperides. The mythographer writes, "Hesperus and Atlas . . . possessed flocks of sheep which excelled in beauty and were in colour of a golden yellow, this being the reason why poets, in speaking of these sheep as *mela* [sheep], called them golden *mela* [apples]." [38] Thus Mercury reminds the hero that

> *Atlas* . . . did present thee
> with the best Sheep, that in his fold were found,
> or golden fruict, on the *hesperian* ground.
>
> (485:173–175)

And scholarship is not out of place in this account, for the relationship between Hercules and the god-turned-mountain has been one of student to teacher. Hercules had rescued "his [Atlas'] faire Daughters: then the prey/ Of a rude *Pirat*." Atlas, in gratitude,

> taught thee all the learning of the Sphere,
> & how, like him, thou mightst the heaven up-beare,
> as that thy labors vertuous recompense.   (485:178–180)

After action the hero has turned to contemplation. But here, as in Sidney's *The Lady of May*, action and contemplation are both parts of the virtuous life; and in the text Jonson gives us, the two merge so that even physical exploits are accomplished by the efforts of the hero's mind.

Turning from past actions to an immediate present, Mercury sets the stage for the dances and revels. Jonson now abandons the hoard of stories surrounding Hercules and attempts some mythmaking of his own. The learned Atlas, it seems, has foretold

> How
> by 'un-alterd law, & working of the stars,
> there should be a cessation of all jars
> 'twixt Vertue, & hir noted opposite,
> Pleasure,   (486:187–191)

and the occasion has now arrived. As the fictive time begins to coincide with an actual evening in 1618, our attention is directed away from the stage to the center of the audience; and the theatrical illusion moves outward to include King James. He becomes Hesperus, Atlas' brother, the evening star. Pleasure and Virtue

> meet here, in the sight
> of Hesperus, the glory of the West,
> the brightest star, that from his burning Crest
> lights all on this side the *Atlantick seas*
> as far as to thy *Pillars Hercules.*   (486:191–195)

The god now gestures directly toward the throne:

> Se where He shines: *Justice,* & *Wisdom* plac'd
> about his *Throne* & those with *Honor* grac'd,
> *Beautie,* & *Love.*   (486:196–198)

This gesture denotes for us the moment at which the masque as an occasional work must justify its existence. Like the dances, the acknowledgment of the royal presence was a basic requirement of the Jonsonian form. And even more than the dances, this moment threatened the validity of the masque-as-poem, tying it to a particular evening and thus transforming the final vision, the world of Ideas, into just another illustration of the sovereignty of Mutability. Moreover, even on the occasional level the moment was a difficult one, since it constituted a scene shift — a radical change in the theatrical illusion — which had to be accomplished not

by the architect but by the poet. We have already examined
Jonson's methods of coping with this problem in a number
of masques. The dangers are represented by *Oberon*, where
the move outward involves the destruction of the theatrical
fiction. For the successes we have *Neptunes Triumph* and
The Gypsies Metamorphos'd, where the joining of masquers
and spectators is not a threat to the masque, but an action
that heightens the illusion and deepens its significance. This
effect is achieved, too, in *Pleasure Reconcild to Vertue.*

Hesperus is, for example, a more satisfactory light in which
to bathe the monarch than that "light scientiall" which
illumined *The Masque of Blacknesse*: James does not have
to *do* anything as the evening star, whereas blackness requires a bleaching agent. Jonson's problem, as we have
already seen, is to include the king in the masque without
investing him with properties that, as a spectator, he cannot
sustain. Here the effect of the allusion to James is, for the
most part, simply to expand the space in which the masque
may be performed. Our attention must now take in not only
the stage, but also what Busino saw as a "fine and spacious
area carpeted all over with green cloth," the dancing floor,
which extended from the proscenium to the royal throne.
In addition, the reference to the monarch ties the masque
to the court in a less obvious way: it allows Jonson to remind us that the chief masquer is also to be the chief courtier:

> this Night
> Vertue brings forth twelve Princes have byn bred
> in this rough *Mountaine,* & neere *Atlas* head,
> the *hill* of *knowledge.* One, & cheif of whom
> of the bright race of *Hesperus* is come,
> Who shall in time the same that He is, be,
> and now is only a lesse Light then He.   (486:201–207)

The allegorization of the audience has been nicely handled
here. We may admire the way *Neptunes Triumph* manages

to include all the spectators in the court the poet has created
around the monarch of the sea, and *Pleasure Reconcild* is
admittedly less ambitious. Nevertheless, it moves beyond its
stage in a way that involves no breach of dramatic decorum,
and the king is made genuinely integral to the masque. Hesperus and Atlas, the center of the court and the exemplar of
wisdom in the fable, are brothers; they have their divinity
in common, but are carefully distinguished from each other.
Gesturing toward the throne, Mercury observes,

> It is not with his Brother
> bearing the world, but ruling such another
> is his renowne.   (486:198–200)

Jonson is invoking a tradition whereby England is conceived
as a separate and specially favored world.[39] It is better to
govern than to serve; Atlas bears his world, but Hesperus
rules his; and the promised resolution of the masque now
becomes simply the proper homage of subject to sovereign.
"Pleasure," explains Mercury, "for his [Hesperus'] delight/
is reconcild to *Vertue*." We are thus prepared at last to
receive the masquers, the twelve princes led by Charles.

For this one evening only, the goddess Virtue trusts these
students of Atlas

> with *Pleasure*, & to theis
> she gives an entraunce to the *Hesperides*,
> faire *Beauties gardens*: neither can she fear
> they should grow soft, or wax effeminat here,
> Since in hir sight, & by hir charge all's don,
> *Pleasure* the Servant, *Vertue* looking on.
>   (486–487:208–213)

The reward for virtue is an entrance to the garden of Hesperus, which by this time we recognize as a pretty periphrasis
for the court. The image of the whole action is therefore a
trope for the masquers' descent to the revels. As we shall

see, Mercury is correct in describing pleasure as the recompense for virtue, and thus uniting both in the dances, but he is only correct on the simplest level. The final reconciliation offered by the masque is rather more ingenious and a great deal more satisfying.

"Here the whole Quire of Musique call the 12 Masquers forth from the Lap of the Mountaine" (lines 214–215). Every action is accompanied by a poetic text in this masque; and the poetry, after all, is for us equivalent to what happens. (In contrast, the poet was unable to express the climactic action of *The Masque of Queenes*, but instead had to describe it.) The spectators are moved into the world of the dance through the operation of Inigo Jones's machinery, and, judging from our one witness, they were quite conscious of what went on behind the scene. "Mount Atlas then opened," writes Busino, "by means of two doors, which were made to turn . . . some gilt columns being placed along either side of the scene, so as to aid the perspective and make the distance seem greater." [40] Our attention, however, is claimed by the poetic experience concomitant with the stage action. The song to which the mountain opens is not merely a textual parallel to a visual effect. Though admittedly it expresses more to a reader than to a spectator, it also functions dramatically. Quite simply, music gets things done in the masque world. It moves us from the expository rhetoric of Mercury into the world of dance. And it spans the gap between verse and choreography by means of lyric poetry, poetry suited to the lyre: the songs of Apollo.

We have already remarked in considering Hercules' victory over the pygmies that the musical consort is a mysterious but highly effective agency. In that episode, it was used to bring about something that could easily have been occasioned by ordinary stage action — for example, one of the pygmies could have struck the hero and awakened him. But the poet has avoided natural causes in much the same way as he has avoided dramatic conflict. The masque moves almost ritualistically through a series of invocations, ceremonies, and what, if we were speaking in religious terms, we would have to call benedictions. This is the pattern the next song follows:

> Ope, aged Atlas, open then thy lap
> and from thy beamy bosom, strike a light,
> that men may read in thy misterious map
> > all lines
> > and signes
> of roial education, and the right.
> > Se how they come, and show
> > that are but borne to know.
> > > Descend,
> > > descend,
> though pleasure lead,
> > feare not to follow:
> they who are bred
> > > within the hill
> > > of skill,
> may safely tread
> > what path they will:
> > no ground of good, is hollow   (487:218–235)

The verse moves with lightness and grace, but also with a sureness which testifies that there is no conflict here between syntax and form. Rhetorically, the song is designed to bring together all elements of the masque, for the revels are about to begin. Three sentences contain the sense: the choir addresses first the scene, then the audience, and finally the masquers.

In the opening lines to Atlas, the masque returns explicitly to questions of knowledge and education. As in Davison's *Proteus*, it is the scenic device, the opening of the rock, that releases the masquers and makes possible the dances. The revels are the justification for Davison's masque, and, in a very literal sense, they are for Jonson's too. But Jonson's poems, and especially the dance poems to follow, serve to explain the previous action with a poetic subtlety and complexity which imply that the devices of mere drama are insufficient. Ultimately, it is lyric verse that must express those "more remov'd mysteries," which were for our poet the true justification of his form. And the opening of the mountain constitutes, in the third line, the revelation of a mystery.

The song is not a complicated one; it achieves both its grace and its clarity by using insistent rhymes with short lines of varied length that carry us through to the end of each sentence, pausing only for full stops and colons at the ends of lines. We may wonder whether any musical setting — the original is now lost — could retain this clarity; indeed, in certain ways the song may even be said to be nonmusical. It is sung as an accompaniment to stage action, yet what it evokes is a literary experience.

This is the first of five poems to deal with the problem of how wisdom is achieved and used. The masquers are Atlas' wards, and what they learn must be acquired and displayed through the movements of the dance. Hercules has learned by experience, and through him we have perceived that the search for virtue and for wisdom lead to the same mountain and the same garden. The spectator learns by observation, but not entirely; for as a courtier he participates in the dance, if only vicariously, through the revels' uniting of masquers and members of the audience. The text, however, addresses itself to a more general public. The mountain opens not so that the dances may begin, but rather

> that men may read in thy misterious map
> all lines
> and signes
> of roial education, and the right.

(The *OED* gives as a common seventeenth-century meaning of "map," "a circumstantial account of a state of things.")

Moreover, we must be aware how little of the song is concerned with the stage action. In fact, only the opening injunction of each sentence recalls us to Whitehall in 1618,
while what follows, treating the theatrical actuality as a
poetic image, goes on as if expounding and elaborating a
metaphor. Virtue's function, says the poem, is the ordering
of pleasure toward a higher end: the order is evident in
the map, the lines and signs, the systematic training implied
by "roial education." The pleasure of these philosopher-
princes contrasts sharply with the god who opened the
masque; for here its function is to serve virtue and reason,
not the sensual appetite. Similarly, "the hill of skill" recalls Comus' claim to invention and looks forward to the
archetype artisan Daedalus, who will enter shortly to lead
the dances. The last line, "No ground of good is hollow,"
may also be relevant to the antimasque. At any rate, the
swiftness with which Hercules' command, "sinck Grove,"
was executed certainly suggests that the ground of that
copse, if it was not hollow, at least contained a trapdoor.
As a moralization, the statement is oracular, and we need
not dwell too long on it. If we do, it will prove — like the
example Socrates offered Meno — to be circular. But it does
manifest a conviction about the moral life which is at the
core of the masque, and which Milton's Lady was shortly to
express in dramatic terms.

Action in this world is effected less by a hero than by the
power of verse and music, which seem to have a life of their
own. Thus it is a song that causes the opening of the mountain. The hero is an exemplar, and we observe him; but in
this masque we reach wisdom not only through observation,
but also through experience, and what we experience is
either dance or poetry. The two forms unite most strik-
ingly in the song we are about to consider. Both are ways
of knowledge, and Hercules has something still to learn. He
becomes a spectator, and his brief interrogation of Mercury

introduces the artist of the revels, the choreographer of
wisdom:

> But *Hermes,* stay a litle: let me pawse.
>   Who's this that leads?
> *Mer.* A Guid[e] that gives them Lawes
>   to all their motions: *Daedalus* the wise;
> *Her.* And doth in sacred harmony comprize
>   his precepts?
> *Mer.* Yes.
> *Her.* They may securely prove
>   then, any laborinth, though it be of *Love.*
>
> (488:241–249)

As the masquers take their places for the first dance, Daedalus
sings:

> Come on, come on; and where you goe,
>   so enter-weave the curious knot,
> as ev'n th'observer scarce may know
>   which lines are Pleasures, and which not.
> First, figure out the doubtful way
>   at which, a while all youth shold stay,
>   where she and Vertue did contend
>   which should have Hercules to frend.
> Then, as all actions of mankind
>   are but a Laborinth, or maze,
>   so let your Daunces be entwin'd,
>   yet not perplex men, unto gaze.
> But measur'd, and so numerous too,
>   as men may read each act you doo.
> And when they see the Graces meet,
>   admire the wisdom of your feet.
> For Daunceing is an exercise
>   not only shews the movers wit,
> but maketh the beholder wise,
>   as he hath powre to rise to it.   (488–489:253–272)

It is, explicitly, "the wisdom of your feet" that the artist
creates here. But, at the same time, the dance is less a fact

for the reader to imagine as best he can than it is a poetic image and a figure of speech. The culmination of the masque is a "curious knot" joining such disparate elements as dance, theater, music and verse in a unity so complex that the revelry of Pleasure and the wisdom of Virtue can no longer be distinguished from each other. The "lines" of line four contribute primarily, of course, to a visual image of the physical bondage that holds the masque together. But they are poetic lines as well; and this half of the ambiguity becomes most significant later, when the dancers are urged to make their movements "measur'd, and so numerous too, / as men may read each act you doo." "Measur'd" can refer to the choreography; a measure is a slow dance, like a pavane. "Measur'd" and "numerous" (consisting of rhythmical units) can both refer to music. But as qualified by the following line, both adjectives become literary terms: the movements are to be ordered and made up of verses. In this way the *reading* of choreography takes on its full meaning, for Daedalus' injunction is to turn the dance into poetry.

Thus the curious knot interweaves the two forms. Its lines carry us back beyond the stage action to that exemplary choice which every man must make alone — "all actions of mankind/ are but a Laborinth or maze" — and then entwine to become the single thread of Ariadne leading us through the artist's creation, the image of life itself. Throughout, the emphasis is on art as a means of organizing and symbolizing experience. The final quatrain completes the masque movement, reaching out into the audience. The dance is a way of knowledge, and "maketh the beholder wise, / as he hath powre to rise to it." The masque has now turned from the education of a prince to the education of an audience. We can rise intellectually to the complex experience the poem has offered. But only the spectator of 1618 could rise literally to join in the revels and thereby turn the poem back into

a dance. It is with this ambiguity that Daedalus concludes
and, through it, leads the masquers into their first display.

When the dance has ended, Daedalus sings again. His second song is about Beauty. Having learned morals, the
masquers are now to study aesthetics. Having proved their
virtue, they are introduced to pleasure:

> O more, & more; this was so well,
>   as praise wants half his voice, to tell;
>   againe yourselves compose,
> and now put all the aptnes on
>   of figure, that proportion
>   or colour can disclose.
> That if those silent arts were lost,
>   Designe, & Picture: they might boast
>   from you a newer ground:
> instructed to the heightning sence
>   of dignitie, and reverence,
>   in your true motions found:
> Begin, begin; for looke, the faire
>   Do longing listen, to what aire
>   you forme your second touch,
> that thei may vent their murmuring hymnes
>   just to the tune you move your limbes,
>   and wish their owne were such.
> Make haste, make haste, for this
>   the Laborinth of *Beautie* is.   (489:276–295)

The verse has become more lyrical, its flow more swift. The
poem is, in fact, more of a song than its predecessor. We hear
more music in it, and it is thereby closer to the dance. Again,
the artisan employs the terminology of another art to describe choreography: we shall notice at once "figure," "proportion," "color"; the dance, to define beauty, becomes "Designe, & Picture," architecture and painting, "silent arts."
But in urging that the dancers "againe yourselves compose,"
Daedalus uses a verb which most commonly describes the
creation of poetry or music — two distinctly audible parts of

the masque. And in providing "a newer ground" for the visual arts, the masquers are creating at once the foundation for "Designe" and the underlying color for "Picture." Most important, however, they are creating the basic melody in a musical composition, which serves as a measure of the skill of both creator and performer. For "the *Ground*," explains Thomas Mace, "is a set Number of *Slow Notes*, very *Grave*, and *Stately*; which, (after It is express'd Once, or Twice, very *Plainly*) then He that hath *Good Brains*, and a *Good Hand*, undertakes to Play several *Divisions* upon It, *Time* after *Time*, till he has shew'd his *Bravery*, both of *Invention*, and *Hand*." [41]

So the dance-as-picture acquires first music and then motion. Daedalus' first song had reached its dance through a kind of intellectual exercise. Here, in contrast, the movement requires the visual and auditory faculties. Figure, proportion, and color are static qualities, and we experience them simply by looking at them. But as the consort plays and the masquers begin their "true motions," not only the lost arts but the listeners and observers too are instructed. At the culmination of the song they are ready to join as active participants in the dance. The poem is an education for the revels, and there is a tone of urgency in it missing from the earlier song. "Begin, begin," the singer calls, interrupting the metaphor he has developed at such length. The artisan of the revels is moving the masque toward its climax. Only in the final line does he return to his visual imagery, but now with a significant difference. A labyrinth is "Designe," but it is also a form one can move through if one knows how. This is the knowledge Daedalus' second dance-poem teaches. And the masquers respond with their second dance.

Indeed, at the end of this "Laborinth of Beautie" the virtuous prince will meet none other than his Ariadne. The third, and Daedalus' last, song presents the revels:

It followes now, you are to prove
　the subtlest maze of all: that's *Love*,
　　and if you stay too long,
　　the fair wil thinck, you do 'em wrong.
Goe choose among — But with a mind
　as gentle as the stroaking wind
　　runs ore the gentler flowres.
And so let all your actions smile,
　as if they meant not to beguile
　　the Ladies, but the howres.
Grace, Laughter, & discourse, may meet,
　and yet, the beautie not goe les:
for what is noble, should be sweet,
　but not dissolv'd in wantonnes.
　　Will you, that I give the law
　　　to all your sport, & some-it?
　　It should be such shold envy draw,
　　　but ever overcome-it.　　　　(490:299–316)

The masque world becomes a society as the dancers acknowledge their partners. The masquer descends, now possessing
the wisdom he has learned in the first dance and the style
he has learned in the second. These meet in social inter-
course; the spectator has been educated too, and the ladies'
beauty is equaled by their attainments. Their dancing is
graceful, they take pleasure in the revels without being "dissolv'd in wantonnes," and they have the qualities of mind
that make their conversation "sweet" to the exemplars of
wisdom and virtue.

The world of the masque is held together by its forms,
which are those of verse and dance. If we consider the masque
as an image of society, as this third song does, the forms of
art become metaphors for those social forms we call manners. Once the partners have been chosen, what happens
changes from stage action to social action. With the revels,
the entertainment is no longer a show, but a game: Daedalus
at last gives "the law/ to all your sport." This transformation in the character of the masque involves a change in the

audience as well. In the first dance, the spectator could "admire the wisdom of your feet"; but here in the third, his reaction is "envy." For the audience is now no longer separated from the image of perfection (and a specifically social perfection, at that) by a proscenium — the dance and all it represents are no longer part of a theatrical illusion, but an evident reality. The viewer envies those of his fellows who join in the revels because, having experienced the masque, he is himself capable of dancing. The dancers must overcome his reaction by inspiring in him the classic response to the appearance of beauty, which is, again, admiration.

But this was also the crucial moment when the king, drunk and sleepy, was inspired only to vent his loud displeasure. It is surely unfair to judge the masquers' success by the royal response. James was not envious, but he *was* petulant and bored; having waited all evening for the revels, he could hardly be happy at seeing the dancers lag. Still, there is a moral to be drawn from this striking display of bad manners by "Hesperus, the glory of the West," and it is simply that, even at the climax of the masque, the world tends to be too much with us. James's "Devil take you all, dance!" [42] must have returned the contemporary audience to the realities of life at court rather abruptly, but it did so only a little earlier than the masque itself. This is the function of the final poem, and Jonson felt it to be so important that he had Mercury speak the entire text before the musicians performed it. Our prose god calls Daedalus and the dancers back to the stage and closes the masque:

> An eye of looking back, were well,
>   or any murmur that wold tell
>   your thoughts, how you were sent,
>   and went,
> to walke with Pleasure, not to dwell.
> Theis, theis are howres, by Vertue spar'd
>   hirself, she being hir owne reward,

But she will have you know,
  that though
hir sports be soft, hir life is hard.
    You must returne unto the Hill,
      and there advance
    with labour, and inhabit still
      that height, and crowne,
    from whence you ever may looke downe
      upon triumphed Chaunce.
She, she it is, in darknes shines.
    'tis she that still hir-self refines,
      by hir owne light, to everie eye,
more seene, more knowne, when Vice stands by.
    And though a stranger here on earth,
      in heaven she hath hir right of birth
        There, there is Vertues seat.
    Strive to keepe hir your owne,
      'tis only she, can make you great,
    though place, here, make you knowne.

(490–491:323–348)

For the princes, the masque is over; they are already looking back on an extraordinary experience. Mercury returns
the masquers to their world and us to ours; both they and we
are left not, as in *The Masque of Queenes*, in a golden age,
but rather in a craggy landscape where "labour," "Chaunce,"
"darknes," "Vice," and the politics of the last line are very
much in evidence. We may even wonder for a moment
whether the "She" who "in darknes shines" is Virtue or the
nearer personification, Chance. The reconciliation of Pleasure and Virtue has been poetically effected through Daedalus'
three songs. By the time we reach the revels, the two figures
have become indistinguishable. "Vertue," the god of information explains for anyone who missed the point the first time,
is "hir owne reward"; and though pleasure has been described
as the princes' recompense, it is finally replaced by its "noted
opposite." This is a darker resolution than Mercury's earlier
one. It implies that there are no rewards except those in-

herent in the virtuous life itself. Jonson the masque writer
retains the sensibility of a satirist. Even the world of the
revels contained envy, and in this final song we can almost
descry whatever local Naxos the princes will choose on which
to abandon their newfound Ariadnes. In any real world, it is
a complicated business for a man to keep his virtue, and with
a full sense of those complexities the masque concludes,
pointing the way back to Jonsonian drama and poetry. Before our eyes now, the scene "closeth, and is a Mountaine
againe, as before." All the masque can do, Jonson seems to
say, is to offer a moment in which a vision of an ideal becomes a poetic and dramatic experience — becomes, in other
words, a reality.

CONCLUSION
MORE REMOVED MYSTERIES

We have now considered the Jonsonian masque in relation to its tradition, its audience, and its theater. From the Tudor disguisings, the Jacobean poet received a form that was primarily spectacular and choreographic. Dialogue, in the early years, was strictly secondary if it appeared at all — we have seen how small the function of the speeches was even in so complex an entertainment as Katherine of Aragon's wedding masque in 1501. But the tradition also included something that made the masque a very special kind of entertainment, and this was the convention of bringing the monarch, and later other members of the audience, into the action of the work. This element, so central to the Jonsonian form, appears in English court entertainments as early as 1377, when a group of masked mummers interrupted a banquet to cast loaded dice with the young Richard II; and Lydgate in 1430 virtually uses Henry VI to conclude a dramatic contention. The court entertainment under Henry VIII changed in character from a show to a game as the king himself danced in the revels; we have traced the development of the Tudor disguising through the works of William Cornysshe and William Crane. *Riches and Love* (1527) displays all the qualities of a mature work of art, and the form developed by Crane remained basically unchanged until Elizabethan times.

It is the discreteness of its parts that most distinctly characterizes the Tudor masque. By 1527, dialogue had clearly become important and even necessary to a form of some complexity. Crane employs three elements in his work: speeches, symbolic action in pantomime, and dance. But he keeps them rigidly separate and unifies the masque by thematic and structural means. His followers under Edward VI and Mary preserved the discreteness more than the unity of the form, and for many years drama and the revels were two different kinds of entertainment. The masque retained its pageants and dances and gave up its dialogue to literature.

It was through literature that the Elizabethan masque continued to develop as a form. William Hunnis employed the basic device of the tradition when, at Kenilworth in 1575, he made Queen Elizabeth an active figure in his drama of the lady of the lake. And in the greatest of the Elizabethan entertainments, Sidney's *The Lady of May*, the monarch was asked — not merely figuratively, but actually — to solve the central contention of the work. Finally, Francis Davison's *Masque of Proteus* attempted to bring together again the parts of the old Tudor disguising by uniting dialogue with dance and by concluding with the revels.

If the type of masque Davison developed looks back to an earlier tradition, it also looks forward to Jonson's work. For the Jacobean poet was deeply concerned with the unity of his form, and he achieved that unity by treating the masques as literature. Jonson transmuted the occasional elements of his commission into integral parts of what was, for him, a poem. We have examined in some detail what constitutes a "successful" Jonsonian masque by looking at both the poet's intentions and his achievement. If *Oberon* is a failure as a masque, it is the failure of a great artist who is still unsure of his form. There is no trace of such uncertainty in *Neptunes Triumph*.

We have considered three masques as steps toward the development of a form in which all elements were integrated into a literary work. Jonson's task as a masque writer was to join a number of totally disparate artistic disciplines; to satisfy the seemingly irreconcilable demands of his audience and his own poetic sense; to merge spectator and actor in a single mimetic illusion. We have seen just how rigidly conventional the form was as he received it. But conventions were his tools; and the way in which he analyzed and used them creatively is as much a triumph of his critical ability as of his theatrical skill.

When a culture accepts the conventions of art without understanding them, the sensibility of the age is in danger of stagnation. The mind then responds not to aesthetic experiences, but to mere formulas, automatically; and the time is ripe for the artist to revitalize both his tradition and his culture through a reinterpretation of the forms of art. Essentially this is what Jonson is doing with the masque. Though he is working on a small scale — the form is unusually rigid, and the audience unusually limited — the problems he encounters are basically the problems of all art. We cannot doubt that, by the time of *Neptunes Triumph*, the masque has become in every sense a viable form.

A striking illustration of the automatic response to art is preserved in Queen Elizabeth's reaction to *The Lady of May*. Sidney's work was a critical examination of convention — in rejecting the shepherd for the forester, he was implying that pastoral was not merely a pleasant romance, but a significant comment on human activity. The queen, however, was too well versed in the convention to follow the poet's argument. Shepherds are the heroes of pastoral, and therefore Espilus must win the lady.

We may consider the dances in a similar light, as a conventional element of the Jacobean masque. When the primary function of the form was to provide an excuse for the revels, the masque in a sense became subservient to its conventions. A notable example is Gascoigne's Montacute en-

tertainment (1572), in which the poet accepts the requirements of his form so uncritically that his avowed purpose
is simply "to devise some verses . . . convenient to render
a good cause of the . . . [masquers'] presence." [1] Davison's
Proteus retains much of this quality, and we find it even in
Jonson's masques of *Blacknesse* and *Queenes*. But Jonson
is clearly moving in a new direction, making a living art
of a set of conventions by using them organically in his
work. And by 1618 he had found a way to make even the
conventional dances functional. At the culmination of *Pleasure Reconcild to Vertue*, they are not only dramatically possible, but structurally necessary.

Not that *Pleasure Reconcild* is the ideal masque-as-poem.
It is rather more diffuse than we, as readers, could wish, and
its verse is occasionally uneven in quality. But in it, nevertheless, Jonson has solved all the basic problems. He no
longer relies on descriptions of setting; there are no gaps
in the text, and no breaches of dramatic decorum. And the
final dance-songs are such striking examples of the Jonsonian
method at its most successful that we may fairly take this
masque as marking the beginning of the great period of his
career that produced *The Gypsies Metamorphos'd* and *Neptunes Triumph* and ended only with the end of the reign.

In other ways, too, *Pleasure Reconcild to Vertue* provides
a useful vantage point from which to survey our study of the
masque form. If we compare it with the solidly realized drama
of *Oberon*, the 1618 work will seem almost a throwback to
the Tudor entertainments. In structure, it is like a pageant;
and though in it Jonson has unified the theatrical and literary
elements, the masque is conceived in sections that are very
nearly as discrete as those of *Riches and Love* had been ninety
years earlier. Interestingly enough, both works also use their
dances in much the same way, as a ballet on a poetically
stated theme. The questions with which the masques are concerned are finally resolved in the revels — the action, that is,

does not simply allow a choreographic conclusion, but requires one. The Jonsonian masque moves away from drama as the antimasque moves toward it.

The ultimate significance of the masque, however, is not defined simply by the antithetical worlds of antimasque and revels. Neither Comus nor Daedalus presides over the court in which we find ourselves at the end of *Pleasure Reconcild to Vertue*. Rather, it is a middle realm, existing somewhere between the extremes of the antimasque's misrule and the revels' order, but including both as possibilities. Indeed, this masque asserts with equal strength both the power of the individual will to overcome disorder and the insubstantiality of the ideal vision. The final song clearly implies the difficulties and uncertainties attendant upon the choice of virtue as a way of life, and Jonson's metaphors provide us with nothing so easy to follow as the conventional pathway. Nevertheless, the choice *is* possible to the resolved mind, and it constitutes the only truly heroic action in the world Jonson has created.

Jonsonian drama presents no image of heroic virtue; but the poetry of the *Epigrammes*, *The Forrest*, and *The Underwood* celebrates numerous figures who have, like Hercules, made the exemplary choice and stand as models to mankind. It is, in fact, in this world and with this kind of heroic potential that the mature Jonsonian masque leaves us. The heroes of Jonson's poetry are — sometimes literally — simply masquers unmasked. Lady Mary Wroth, a nymph in *The Masque of Blacknesse*, thus becomes a prototype of womanly virtue, capable of replacing the traditional sources of poetic inspiration:

> Madame, had all antiquitie beene lost,
> All historie seal'd up, and fables crost;
> That we had left us, nor by time, nor place,
> Least mention of a *Nymph*, a *Muse*, a *Grace*,

But even their names were to be made a-new,
Who could not but create them all, from you? [2]

Jonson then presents her, appropriately disguised, as several mythological figures:

He, that but saw you wear the wheaten hat,
Would call you more then CERES, if not that:
And, drest in shepheards tyre, who would not say:
You were the bright OENONE, FLORA, or *May*?
If dancing, all would cry th'*Idalian* Queene,
Were leading forth the *Graces* on the greene:
And, armed to the chase, so bare her bow
DIANA'alone, so hit, and hunted so.
There's none so dull, that for your stile would aske,
That saw you put on PALLAS plumed caske:
Or, keeping your due state, that would not cry,
There JUNO sate, and yet no Peacock by.
So are you *Natures Index*, and restore,
I'your selfe, all treasure lost of th'age before.

Here, as in the masque, the disguise is only an expression of the inner reality. It is what establishes the figure as a valid symbol, making of the heroine "Natures Index," in whom all the lost virtues are preserved. But at the same time, the disguise also serves to convey those virtues to a world of spectators, and thereby to recreate in the present the heroism of the past.

Similarly, to the Countess of Bedford — another nymph in the masques of *Blacknesse* and *Beautie* and a queen in *The Masque of Queenes* — Jonson not only gives all the social graces, but allows her to be untouched by the vicissitudes of sublunary life:

a learned, and a manly soule
I purpos'd her; that should, with even powers,
The rock, the spindle, and the sheeres controule
Of destinie, and spin her owne free houres.[3]

Sir William Roe, returning from a journey, has the character of a classic hero:

> This is that good AENEAS, past through fire,
> Through seas, stormes, tempests: and imbarqu'd for hell,
> Came back untouch'd.[4]

And Sir Lucius Cary and Sir Henry Morison, in the great ode written near the end of Jonson's career, become explicit heroic examples in a world that barely makes room for virtue:

> You liv'd to be the great surnames,
> And titles, by which all made claimes
> Unto the Vertue. Nothing perfect done,
> But as a CARY, or a MORISON.
> And such a force the faire example had,
> As they that saw
> The good, and durst not practise it, were glad
> That such a Law
> Was left yet to Man-kind.[5]

Such figures fill the poems, safeguarding the classic truths in a society that has forgotten them. They embody the ideals of the masque in settings that suggest the plays.

There is one particularly striking instance where the masque itself is included in Jonson's poetic vision. In the epistle to Sir Robert Wroth,[6] the hero's moral choice is seen in the traditional terms of the rejection of a court world for a pastoral idyll:

> How blest art thou, canst love the countrey, WROTH,
>   Whether by choice, or fate, or both;
> And, though so neere the citie, and the court,
>   Art tane with neithers vice, nor sport.   (lines 1-4)

Here, ironically, the masque, reduced to its most momentary and spectacular aspects, exemplifies the vices of society, and provides a center for Jonson's satiric comment:

> Nor throng'st (when masquing is) to have a sight
>   Of the short braverie of the night;
> To view the jewells, stuffes, the paines, the wit
>   There wasted, some not paid for yet!

> But canst, at home, in thy securer rest,
>   Live, with un-bought provision blest.   (lines 9–14)

The poem then modulates into the richness of a pastoral landscape, equally artificial, but also fruitful and lasting:

> Among'st the curled woods, and painted meades,
>   Through which a serpent river leades
> To some coole, courteous shade, which he calls his,
>   And makes sleepe softer then it is! . . .
> The whil'st, the severall seasons thou has seene
>   Of flowrie fields, of cop'ces greene,
> The mowed meddowes, with the fleeced sheepe,
>   And feasts, that either shearers keepe;
> The ripened eares, yet humble in their height,
>   And furrows laden with their weight;
> The apple-harvest, that doth longer last;
>   The hogs return'd home fat from mast;
> The trees cut out in log; and those boughes made
>   A fire now, that lent a shade!   (lines 17–46)

Here, within the pastoral world, the masque is summoned up again. Now it is an expression of order and bounty, and it relates the virtuous man to whatever is mythical and divine:

> COMUS puts in, for new delights;
> And fills thy open hall with mirth, and cheere,
>   As if in SATURNES raigne it were;
> APOLLO's harpe, and HERMES lyre resound,
>   Nor are the *Muses* strangers found:
> The rout of rurall folke come thronging in,
>   (Their rudenesse then is thought no sinne)
> Thy noblest spouse affords them welcome grace;
>   And the great *Heroes*, of her race,
> Sit mixt with losse of state, or reverence.   (lines 48–57)

The hosts have, with the entrance of the gods, become a race of heroes. Comus is not a villain in this setting, and the appearance of "the rout of rurall folk" — like the cook's antimasque of sailors in *Neptunes Triumph* — is here "thought no sinne." In fact, both appetite and rudeness, natural simplicity and good humor, belong to this life. It is the city (on which the masque is "wasted," a mere diversion) that denies and destroys what is human, and from which nature is excluded:

> Let this man sweat, and wrangle at the barre,
>   For every price, in every jarre,
> And change possessions, oftner with his breath,
>   Then either money, warre, or death:
> Let him, then hardest sires, more disinherit,
>   And each where boast it as his merit,
> To blow up orphanes, widdowes, and their states;
>   And thinke his power doth equall *Fates*.
> Let that goe heape a masse of wretched wealth,
>   Purchas'd by rapine, worse then stealth,
> And brooding o're it sit, with broadest eyes,
>   Not doing good, scarce when he dyes.
> Let thousands more goe flatter vice, and winne,
>   By being organes to great sinne,
> Get place, and honor, and be glad to keepe
>   The secrets, that shall breake their sleepe:
> And, so they ride in purple, eate in plate,
>   Though poyson, thinke it a great fate.
>
> (lines 73–90)

This might be an anthology of evils from Jonsonian comedy and represents the realities with which the hero is faced. But the hero, in such poems as this, has a more evident and more important kind of reality even than the world of Jonson's satire: he has the reality of the masquer, the nobleman beneath the symbolic disguise, who is capable of learning, choosing, and acting. It is such figures, steadfast in a world of vice, misrule, and decay, who provide the links between the ideal vision of Jonsonian masque and the satiric vision of Jonsonian drama.

Drama exists in time: things happen and characters act on each other. Conversely, the world of the volatile and spectacular masque is a world of ideas, untouched by change. Often, as the antimasque is banished, we hear an invocation to the forces of nature to stay their motion; and the scene is lifted out of time. The end of *Love Freed from Ignorance and Folly* makes explicit the value of this poetic device:

> What just excuse had aged *Time*,
>   His wearie limbes now to have eas'd,
> And sate him downe without his crime,
>   While every thought was so much pleas'd!
> For he so greedie to devoure
>   His owne, and all that hee brings forth,
> Is eating every piece of houre
>   Some object of the rarest worth.
> Yet this is rescued from his rage
> As not to die by time, or age.

The poet's very concern that the masque be valid as literature has been metaphorically incorporated into the work.

I remarked in an earlier chapter that, in the two late masques written for King Charles, Jonson was unable to transmute the occasional elements into poetry, and I have suggested some reasons for their comparative failure as literature. To recapitulate briefly, both *Loves Triumph Through Callipolis* and *Chloridia* are essentially accounts of theatrical spectacles, with occasional dialogue and song. Although what verse they contain is often excellent, the form is clearly no longer the poet's. So marked is the ascendancy of architect and choreographer over the aging Jonson that the antimasque of *Loves Triumph* includes no text at all. The poet's function was now to provide a description of a work conceived largely in visual terms, and he vented his dissatisfaction with this new position in the famous expostulation.[7]

> O Showes! Showes! Mighty Showes!
> The Eloquence of Masques! What need of prose
> Or Verse, or Sense t'express Immortall you?
> You are the Spectacles of State!

In *Pleasure Reconcild*, we saw how effectively Jonson could use literary terminology to express the other elements of the masque. Here the same device is employed for satiric ends; but the irony of "The Eloquence of Masques!" implies all too clearly that the poet is out of a job. The form has new conventions, the audience new expectations:

> Oh, to make Boardes to speake! There is a task!
> Painting and Carpentry are the Soule of Masque!
> Pack with your pedling Poetry to the Stage!
> This is the money-gett, Mechanick Age!

Jonson — and not Jonson alone — has been replaced by Jones, the master-surveyor,

> The maker of the Propertyes! in summe
> The Scene! The Engine! but he now is come
> To be the Musick-Master! Fabler too!
> He is, or would be the mayne Dominus doe
> All in the Worke!

We have already looked at the circumstances surrounding Jonson's return to the stage. It is hardly surprising that the return was not a triumphant one, for both external considerations and the poet's own development worked against a new dramatic success. *The Staple of Newes*, produced in 1626, was Jonson's first play in ten years; its appearance nearly coincided with the coronation of King Charles. We may assume that between Twelfth Night 1625, when the old king's court witnessed *The Fortunate Isles*, and February 1626, when the new king's servants performed *The Staple of Newes*, Jonson gained a good notion of what he might expect at the Whitehall of Charles and Henrietta Maria. But the conventions of the stage and the expectations of the viewers were no longer what they had been fifteen years earlier, the time of the poet's greatest dramatic successes — nor could Jonson have written another *Alchemist* if he had wished. His art had moved beyond the great plays of the decade before 1614, and we shall be ignoring the evidence of the masques and the poetry if we decide that it had not progressed.

To put the case in very simple terms, during the period when Jonson was creating his court entertainments, he was also creating an audience for them. As we have seen, the masques show a remarkable comprehension of the demands of that audience — of all his rivals at court, Jonson alone was regularly commissioned to produce the Twelfth-Night entertainment — and it is a comprehension that grows in depth and subtlety over the years. If we think of Jonson as primarily a court poet and scholar after 1616, we shall not find it strange that he should have been less in touch with the interests of the paying spectator than with those of what was essentially a captive audience. But this is only part of the story. In the last decade of the old reign, Jonson's dramatic art developed entirely through the masque form. And the concept of theater that crystallized in the masque had also made the drama rigid.

The masque is a world of absolutes, in which all action is inherent in the nature of the individual figures. What we would call the drama of the form (what happens on stage) is predetermined by the structure of such a world: we have examined an extreme case in *The Masque of Queenes*, where Good banishes Evil without even a confrontation. I have briefly suggested that the same tendency is apparent in Jonsonian comedy; for the humors theory supposes that characteristics determine action, and thus what a character will do is as much a part of his nature as the particular humor that makes him a subject for comedy. Roughly, then, there are two kinds of people in the "normal" Jonsonian comedy: the cheats and the cheated. These two fit in with each other as gears in a machine; when they are made to mesh, the play begins to move. Yet, of course, drama involves interaction of characters, conflict — a condition, in short, in which the gears cease to mesh and the play's predetermined movement is violated. Thus, for example, the central action of *The Alchemist* is built around a fight between Subtle and Face, a situation in which one figure refuses to fulfill the role ordained for him. I have grossly oversimplified what is in Jonson's hands a complex and malleable form. Nevertheless, the concept is basic to all Jonsonian comedy.

But Jonsonian comedy is satire — so, indeed, is Jonsonian tragedy — and the masque has different ends. If in the humors plays characteristics are absolutes, they are only absolutes on the human scale. There are fools and there are swindlers; but the figures of Virtue, Beauty, Fame, that fill the masques and are intermittently visible in the poems are largely missing from the plays. To a satirist, of course, it is human vice that is eternal, but vice is as absent from the world of the revels as virtue is from the drama. In a sense, Jonson produced the best masques because he had produced the best humors comedies: the courtly form shows us the humors theory applied to universals.

The difficulty with the late plays is that the violation of the movement I have described as mechanical never takes place. The fantastic complexity of the plot of *The New Inne* (1629) only testifies to the trouble Jonson was having in getting anything to happen on stage; the play remains a collection of characters, and not very clearly drawn characters at that. It seems obvious that, for a dramatist experiencing this sort of difficulty, the masque provided not only an ideal solution, but a medium in which he had a freer hand. As we have seen throughout our consideration of the form, whatever happens in the masque happens not so much between the characters themselves as between the characters and the viewers. Jonson sees the revels as the moment when the masquer breaks through the limits of his stage, when the illusion moves out into the audience. This is the point toward which the action of the masque moves, and there could be no such climax in a play.

Nevertheless, there are analogous elements in Jonson's drama. It is a commonplace to say that the plays tend to be self-conscious — we are constantly being presented with characters who comment on the action, with plays within plays, with critical inductions and epilogues to explain the drama. The *point* of a drama, Shakespeare might have objected, is that it acts out its meaning, and no explanation can do it justice. And yet, as early as *Every Man Out of His Humour* (1599), Jonson was experimenting with nondramatic means of getting closer to his audiences — and critics. After a brief opening dialogue, Asper looks out into the Globe theater:

> I not observ'd this thronged round till now.
> Gracious and kind spectators, you are welcome,
>
> (I.i.51–52)

and he continues to expound the purpose of the play he is presenting. He even provides stand-ins for an audience he cannot bring on stage:

> What? are you ready there! MITIS sit downe:
> And my CORDATUS. Sound hough, and begin.
> I leave you two, as censors, to sit here:
> Observe what I present, and liberally
> Speake your opinions, upon every Scene,
> As it shall passe the view of these spectators.
>
> (I.i.151–156)

This is undeniably a way for the playwright to move closer to his viewers, but paradoxically it also keeps the viewers at a considerable distance from the dramatic action. In the great comedies, Jonson manages to effect the necessary rapport through the more usual means of dramatic irony. But in the later plays, the move off stage has become all-important; it is as if the poet can no longer express himself through drama. *The Magnetick Lady*, which one would think was clear enough, has not only an induction but an explanatory chorus to conclude every act except the last. *The New Inne*, which proved incomprehensible to its first — and last — contemporary audience, had to be provided with arguments not only of the whole play but of each act individually, with even a note marking the point where "the Epitasis, or businesse of the Play" begins (incidentally, it does not begin until the third act), and a list of the dramatis personae "With some short Characterisme of the chiefe Actors."

These brief notes should suggest in what way the masques are a link between the playwright of *Volpone* and that of *The New Inne*. The idea of theater that Jonson conceived, he could perfect only in the masque. The unmediated confrontation of actor and spectator was impossible in the playhouse, though the conventions of French drama came closer to allowing it than did the English. Thus Molière's miser, Harpagon, can turn to the audience and beg for information of the thief who has robbed him. This is, admittedly, an atypical instance: even French characters do not generally go quite this far. But if we wish more usual examples, we have only to consider the ease and frequency with which Molière brings a single actor on stage to explain his intentions or feelings. Such a scene has the quality of an extended aside; in contrast, the Elizabethan soliloquy is a more formal device, usually the place for some very serious thinking. Neither one actually acknowledges the audience, though often the French dramatist, without breaking the framework of the play's illusion, does directly involve the spectator in the stage action.

For example, in *L'Ecole des Femmes*, Arnolphe's remarks on husbands are strictly relevant to the dramatic situation, but they are also obviously pronounced with an oblique gesture toward the audience: "Fort bien: est il au monde une autre ville aussi / Où il ait des maris si patients qu'ici?" Arnolphe is not, like a Jonsonian explicator, speaking out of context; he is not a chorus, but a character. We see the flaws in his reasoning, just as his friend Chrysalde does, and thus the playwright gives us the same reality as he has given his stage figures. We have also seen this quality achieved by Sidney in *The Lady of May*, and by Jonson himself in the opening of *Love Restored*, through the use of direct addresses to the audience. We might briefly contrast the effect of an Elizabethan soliloquy on the spectator. Prince Hal's revelation, "I know you all, and will awhile uphold / The unyok'd humour of your idleness," tells us things about him that no other mere character can know. The soliloquy enables us to see into the speaker; it gives him another dimension, a depth of a sort that is, on the whole, alien to the characters of comedy. Hal exposes his motives, and, though we may not approve, we understand and sympathize. Arnolphe exposes his motives, and we understand and criticize. If we see into Hal, we see through Arnolphe. In Hal's case, we are in collusion with a character; in Arnolphe's, with the author.

As a concluding note, it is interesting to remark that what I have defined as the masque movement has borne fruit in the modern theatre. Jonson's age was developing conventions of the stage and the nature of the illusion it contains that have persisted until the present century. If the Jacobean poet was to see the climax of his work as a point at which the actor broke through the limits of his stage, those limits had to be very firmly defined. Thus, Inigo Jones regularly used the proscenium arch for masques, though not for plays,[8] and through the use of perspective stressed visual realism in his settings. It is this illusion of reality that the masque is able to extend out into its audience. But, placed on such a stage, the drama had to remain behind its proscenium; and we may date the end of the Shakespearean age in the theater from the time when a masque setting could also contain the action of a play. The necessity for scenic realism precludes the fluidity attained by Shakespeare's drama, with its frequent short scenes and changes of location. Even so simple a convention as the soliloquy, which was perfectly unexceptionable in an Elizabethan playhouse, is troublesome on a realistic stage where we have a tendency to see a man alone talking to himself. Burbage's Hamlet was far closer to his viewers than Garrick's. But our own age is beginning to conceive of another kind of theater. Pirandello's actors cannot quite merge with their audience as did the Tudor masquers when they unmasked; but they come very close to it when, in *Tonight We Improvise*, they appear and chat in the theater lobby during intermission. Thornton Wilder uses his stage manager in *Our Town* as a similar means to more conventional ends. Indeed, we could choose examples ranging from Chekhov to Adamov. If the drama is approaching its audience again after three hundred years, it must have something to say that cannot be expressed from behind a proscenium wall. No longer confronted by an illusion of reality, we may find, like the courtly spectator at the moment of the revels, that the world of theater is one in which we play a new kind of part.

NOTES

INDEX

NOTES

PART I. THE METAMORPHOSES OF PROTEUS

1. *Ben Jonson* [Works], ed. C. H. Herford and Percy and Evelyn Simpson, 11 vols. (Oxford, 1925–1952), VIII, 735. All Jonson quotations are from this edition, hereafter cited as *Jonson*.

2. E. K. Chambers, ed., *Aurelian Townshend's Poems and Masks* (Oxford, 1912), p. 83.

3. *The Court Masque* (Cambridge, Eng., 1927), pp. 166–167.

4. John Nichols, *The Progresses . . . of Queen Elizabeth*, 2nd ed. (London, 1823), II, 159.

5. Quoted in *Jonson*, X, 448.

6. *The Court Masque*, p. 178.

7. *Discourses* (1673 ed.), p. 215. Quoted by Basil Willey, *The Seventeenth Century Background* (New York, 1953), p. 153.

8. One example is Gascoigne's Montacute masque (1572), discussed below, which he included in his published works.

9. Nichols, *Progresses*, III, 262–263.

10. *Ibid.*, p. 298.

11. Sir Walter Greg, ed., *Gesta Grayorum 1688*, Malone Society Reprints (Oxford, 1914), p. 67.

12. See, e.g., Allardyce Nicoll, *Stuart Masques and the Renaissance Stage* (London, 1937), p. 59.

13. *The Works of Lucian*, tr. H. W. and F. G. Fowler (Oxford, 1905), II, 245.

14. The text is ambiguous about the number of attendants and which of them were the musicians. I have adopted the interpretation of E. K. Chambers, *The Elizabethan Stage* (Oxford, 1923), IV, 56.

15. Campion's *Works*, ed. Percival Vivian (Oxford, 1909), p. 352. Except for this song, my text of the masque is a composite made by comparing the version in *Gesta Grayorum* (London, 1688) with the manuscript copy in MS. Harley 541. Both are reprinted in Greg's *Gesta Grayorum 1688*.

16. Numbers in parentheses are line references to the text of the work in Greg's edition, pp. 57ff, hereafter cited as *Gesta*.

17. There is an interesting exception in *Love Restored*, where the villainy of the antimasquer hinges on his impersonation of a masquer.

18. *The Faerie Queene*, II.iv.10–11.

19. In MS. Harley 541. See *Gesta*, p. vii.

20. MS. Harley 247, f. 172v. Quoted by Paul Reyher, *Les Masques Anglais* (Paris, 1909), p. 499.

21. John Lydgate, *The Minor Poems*, ed. H. N. MacCracken (London, 1934), II, 675. Numbers in parentheses are line references to this text.

22. In MS. Harley 69. Quoted by Reyher, pp. 500–502. I have adopted the standard sixteenth-century spelling of the queen's name.

23. Edward Halle, "The Triumphant Reigne of Kyng Henry the VIII," in *The Union of . . . Lancaster and York*, 2nd ed. (London, 1550), f. xvi.r.(c4r.). (The pagination in Halle is not continuous from section to section.)

24. *Les Masques Anglais*, pp. 18–28, 491–494.

25. Halle, f. xvi.r.(c4r.).

26. *Ibid.*, f. xxii.v.(d4v.).

27. *Ibid.*, f. clvii.v.(D1v.).

28. *Ibid.*, f. clviii.r.(D2r.).

29. Another very interesting account of the same masque is found in *Calendar of State Papers (Venetian)*, ed. Rawdon Brown (London, 1871), IV, 59, a letter from the Venetian secretary in London, Gasparo Spinelli. It adds a good deal of incidental detail and some introductory material to the dialogue that Halle omits. Unfortunately, it also adds a good deal of confusion; Spinelli appears not to have understood the point of the debate and treats the masquing simply as a group of elaborate dances.

30. J. S. Brewer, ed., *Letters and Papers . . . of Henry VIII* (London, 1864), vol. II, part 2, p. 1501.

31. A full discussion will be found in C. W. Wallace, *The Evolution of the English Drama* (Berlin, 1912), pp. 48ff.

32. *Ibid.*, p. 74.

33. *Ibid.*, p. 83.

34. E. K. Chambers, *The Medieval Stage* (Oxford, 1903), I, 406.

35. *The Posies*, ed. J. W. Cunliffe (Cambridge, Eng., 1907), p. 75.

36. Robert Laneham, *Letter . . .* , ed. F. J. Furnivall (London, 1907), p. 33.

37. George Gascoigne, *Works*, ed. J. W. Cunliffe (Cambridge, Eng., 1910), vol. II. Numbers in parentheses are page references to this edition.

38. Laneham, p. 34. The episode as originally conceived was far more elaborate, and the queen took a more active part. See Gascoigne's summary, *Works*, II, 106.

39. "Herdsman of the seas" is a conventional epithet for Proteus, common in both classical and Elizabethan literature. E.g., "Proteus is Shepheard of the seas of yore," *Faerie Queene*, III.viii.30.

40. Laneham, pp. 34–35.

41. The text used is that of Albert Feuillerat, ed., *The Complete Works of Sir Philip Sidney*, II (Cambridge, Eng., 1922), 329–338. For convenience, numbers in parentheses are page references to this edition.

W. A. Ringler's authoritative text of the *Poems* (Oxford, 1962) differs from Feuillerat's only in minor points of punctuation in the final song.

42. Cf. p. 329: "I dare stay here no longer, for our men say in the countrey, the sight of you is infectious."

43. The disguised Musidorus, in *Arcadia*, II.3, embodies the identical conceit in verse: "My sheepe are thoughts, which I both guide and serve." Feuillerat, *Sidney*, I (1912) 163–164.

44. See Mary S. Steele, *Plays and Masques at Court* (New Haven, 1926), pp. 114, 119–120, 125.

PART II. TO MAKE THE SPECTATORS UNDERSTANDERS

1. "The Jonsonian Masque as a Literary Form," *Journal of English Literary History*, XXII (June 1955), 123.

2. "The Interpretation of Jonson's Courtly Spectacles," *PMLA*, LXI (June 1946), 473.

3. *Tamburlaine*, part 1, lines 3980–3982.

4. Spectators were traditionally permitted to dismantle the scenery and properties at the conclusion of such productions.

5. Page and line references are to the text of the masques in Herford and Simpson's *Jonson*, vol. VII.

6. Allardyce Nicoll, *Stuart Masques and the Renaissance Stage* (London, 1937), p. 34.

7. A valuable discussion of this aspect of the Jonsonian masque will be found in W. Todd Furniss, "Ben Jonson's Masques," in *Three Studies in the Renaissance* (New Haven, 1958), pp. 89–177.

8. *Jonson*, I, 143.

9. Quoted in *Jonson*, X, 448, 449.

10. *The Court Masque* (Cambridge, Eng., 1927), p. 268.

11. The only substantial exception is *The Masque of Augurs* (1622). There are a few small notes to *Neptunes Triumph* (1624).

12. *Jonson*, I, 231.

13. *Ibid.*, I, 205.

14. Quoted by G. E. Bentley, *The Jacobean and Caroline Stage* (Oxford, 1941–1956), IV, 646.

15. *Ibid.*, IV, 647.

16. *Jonson*, I, 96. See also "The Humble Petition of Poore Ben. to . . . King Charles," *The Underwood*, lxxvi.

17. Bentley, IV, 671.

18. Letters to Carleton from Brent, Sir Edward Harwood, Sir Edward Sherburne, John Chamberlain. All are quoted by Bentley, IV, 670–671.

19. *Ibid.*, p. 672.

20. *Ibid.*, p. 671.

21. *Jonson*, I. 72.

22. Cf. the rhetoric of Zeal-of-the-Land Busy in *Bartholomew Fair*.

23. *Jonson*, I, 90.

24. Bentley, IV, 841.

25. *Jonson*, I, 90–91.

26. Bentley, IV, 652.

27. Mary S. Steele, *Plays and Masques at Court* (New Haven, 1926), pp. 231–236.

28. Reyher, *Les Masques Anglais*, pp. 528–529.

29. *Blacknesse*, lines 90–92.

30. *Loves Triumph Through Callipolis*, lines 46–50.

31. Jonson had a brief moment of revenge. His last masque, *Love's Welcome at Bolsover* (1634), was not commissioned by King Charles, and in it Jonson was for once free of Inigo Jones. The poet celebrates his restoration by creating an antimasque around his antagonist, who appears as an outrageous architect named Iniquo Vitruvius. The work is clearly not in the style of Jonson's two Caroline masques, but is rather an obvious attempt to revive the Jacobean form. If Jonson intended it not as vengeance but as a final bid for royal favor, it must have seemed a remarkably inept one. Charles was, understandably, not enchanted with it.

32. *Cynthias Revells*, V.vi.1.

33. *Jonson*, X, 527.

34. *For the Honour of Wales*, lines 371ff. "Charles James Stuart" is not Prince Charles, but King James. Cf. William Camden on anagrams: "To begin with his most Excellent Majestie our dread Soveraigne, was made this declaring his undoubted rightfull claime to the Monarchy of Britain, as the successor of the valourous king Arthur. *Charles James Steuart* / CLAIMES ARTHURS SEATE As this is also truly verified in his person" (*Remaines* . . . , London, 1605, p. 153). Herford and Simpson note the reference, but incorrectly give the page as 171.

35. There is a mountain in Wales popularly called Arthur's Chair. Possibly Jonson is also alluding through it to Henry's investiture as Prince of Wales.

36. Quoted in *Jonson*, X, 665.

37. *Jonson*, II, 326.

38. "Of real business of the state they know nothing, and they are as mute as fishes about it. But this does not prevent their talking about the affairs of state and poisoning the news as the breath of the eater of garlic poisons the air." *Jonson*, X, 667.

39. Beaumont and Fletcher, *Works*, ed. A. R. Waller (Cambridge, Eng., 1912), X, 379.

40. Preface, *The Vision of the Twelve Goddesses*, in *The Complete Works . . . of Samuel Daniel*, ed. A. B. Grosart (London, 1885), III, 196, lines 268ff.

41. Thomas Campion, *Works*, ed. Percival Vivian (Oxford, 1909), p. 76.

42. Herford and Simpson in *Jonson*, II, 261.

43. *Ibid.*

44. *Conversations*, line 55. Jonson said "Fletcher and Chapman," but so far as we know, Fletcher wrote no masques. Herford and Simpson suggest that Drummond is misreporting a reference to Beaumont and explain, "the point of the remark . . . is that Daniel and Campion could not write masques" (I, 155). They do not explain why, except for the fact that Jonson and Beaumont were friends, Jonson should have approved of Beaumont's masque writing and not of Campion's.

45. Quoted by Welsford, *The Court Masque*, p. 257.

46. *Ibid.*, p. 254.

47. "The Interpretation of Jonson's Courtly Spectacles," *PMLA*, LXI (June 1946), 473.

48. *Ben Jonson and the Language of Prose Comedy* (Cambridge, Mass., 1960), p. 244. Barish's chapter on the masque is suggestive and extremely valuable.

PART III. THE TRANSFORMATION SCENE

1. Quoted in *Jonson*, X, 448.

2. *The Masque of Blacknesse*, line 91.

3. References so noted are to *Jonson*, vol. VII.

4. Allardyce Nicoll, *Stuart Masques and the Renaissance Stage* (London, 1937), p. 39.

5. Lily B. Campbell, *Scenes and Machines on the English Stage* (Cambridge, Eng., 1923), p. 167.

6. For a general discussion, see John C. Meagher, "The Dance and the Masques of Ben Jonson," *Journal of the Warburg and Courtauld Institute*, vol. XXV, no. 3–4 (1962), pp. 258–277.

7. *Hymn in Honour of Beautie*, lines 132–133.

8. M. C. Bradbrook, *The Growth and Structure of Elizabethan Comedy* (London, 1955), p. 187.

9. *Ibid.*

10. *Jonson*, I, 133.

11. Letter to Raleigh, *Faerie Queene*, ed. J. C. Smith (Oxford, 1909), II, 486.

12. *Jonson*, I, 132.

13. Otto Gombosi, "Some Musical Aspects of the English Court Masque," *Journal of the American Musicological Society*, I (Fall 1948), 3.

14. Quoted by Bentley, IV, 670–671.

15. A. B. Hinds, ed., *Calendar of State Papers (Venetian)*, XV (London, 1909), 112. The letter is reprinted in the original Italian in *Jonson*, X, 58off.

16. *Elizabethan Poetry* (Cambridge, Mass., 1952), p. 293. Smith's entire discussion of the significance of the figure of Hercules to the English Renaissance (pp. 293ff) is excellent and very much to the point.

17. *Memorabilia*, II.i.21–34.

18. *Choice of Emblemes* (Leyden, 1586), p. 40.

19. Bacon writes, "*Dancing to Song*, is a Thing of great State, and Pleasure. . . . *Acting in Song*, especially in Dialogues, hath an extreme Good Grace: I say *Acting*, not *Dancing*, (For that is a Meane and Vulgar Thing . . .)" ("Of Masques and Triumphs"). The distinction is interesting: Bacon praises dancing to the accompaniment of music — both the masque dances and revels — and opera, but dancing "*in* song" (while singing), a traditional part of the popular jig, had no place in good society.

20. *The Renaissance and English Humanism* (Toronto, 1939), p. 108.

21. *English Literature in the Earlier Seventeenth Century* (Oxford, 1945), p. 365.

22. Philostratus, *Imagines*, tr. Arthur Fairbanks (London, 1931), pp. 9–13.

23. *Le Imagini de i Dei degli Antichi* (Lyons, 1581), p. 347.

24. Philostratus, *Les Images*, tr. Blaise de Vigenère (Paris, n.d. [1614]), p. 9. Isaac's engraving is dated 1613.

25. *Le Imagini*, p. 346.

26. *Ibid.*, p. 348.

27. *Comus*, line 776.

28. *Viridarium Hieroglyphico-Morale* . . . (Frankfurt, 1619), p. 132.

29. *The Symbolic Persons in the Masques of Ben Jonson* (Durham, N.C., 1948), pp. 69–70.

30. *State Papers* (*Venetian*), XV, 112.

31. Either the antimasque and the fight took place simultaneously — and when Hercules finished with Antaeus he moved on to stop the reveling — or else the dance started again briefly after being interrupted by the pantomime. In any case, Hercules' opening lines indicate that the "various and most extravagant antics" are in progress after his battle has ended.

32. *Queenes*, lines 354–355.

33. *Imagines*, p. 229.

34. *State Papers* (*Venetian*) XV, 112.

35. *Ibid.*

36. Cf. Jonson's "Epode" (*The Forrest*, XI), esp. lines 13–30.

37. Cf. an interesting parallel from Blake's *Milton*: "I will not cease from Mental Fight, / Nor shall my Sword sleep in my hand." The weapon only needs to be *awake* for its purpose to be accomplished.

38. Diodorus Siculus, *The Library of History*, tr. C. H. Oldfather (Cambridge, Mass., 1935), II, 429.

39. For a general discussion of the tradition, see J. W. Bennett, "Britain Among the Fortunate Isles," *Studies in Philology*, LIII (April 1956), 114–140.

40. *State Papers* (*Venetian*), XV, 112.

41. Thomas Mace, *Musick's Monument* (London, 1676), p. 129.
42. *State Papers (Venetian)*, XV, 113.

CONCLUSION. MORE REMOVED MYSTERIES

1. *The Posies*, ed. J. W. Cunliffe (Cambridge, Eng., 1907), p. 75.
2. "To Mary Lady Wroth," *Epigrammes*, cv, lines 1–6.
3. "On Lucy Countesse of Bedford," *Epigrammes*, lxxvi, lines 13–16.
4. "To William Roe," *Epigrammes*, cxxviii, lines 12–14.
5. "To . . . Sir Lucius Cary, and Sir H. Morison," *The Underwood*, lxx, lines 113–121.
6. "To Sir Robert Wroth," *The Forrest*, iii.
7. "An Expostulacion with Inigo Jones," lines 39–65.
8. See E. K. Chambers, *The Elizabethan Stage* (Oxford, 1923), I, 234.

INDEX